David Crystal

50 Questions about English Usage

Cambridge Handbooks for Language Teachers

This series, now with over 50 titles, offers practical ideas, techniques and activities for the teaching of English and other languages, providing inspiration for both teachers and trainers.

The Pocket Editions come in a handy, pocket-sized format and are crammed full of tips and ideas from experienced English language teaching professionals, to enrich your teaching practice.

Recent titles in this series:

David Crystal's 50 Questions about English Usage

David Crystal

Consultant and editor: Scott Thornbury

CAMBRIDGE
UNIVERSITY PRESS

University Printing House, Cambridge CB2 8BS, United Kingdom

One Liberty Plaza, 20th Floor, New York, NY 10006, USA

477 Williamstown Road, Port Melbourne, VIC 3207, Australia

314–321, 3rd Floor, Plot 3, Splendor Forum, Jasola District Centre,
New Delhi – 110025, India

103 Penang Road, #05-06/07, Visioncrest Commercial, Singapore 238467

Cambridge University Press is part of the University of Cambridge.

It furthers the University's mission by disseminating knowledge in the pursuit of
education, learning and research at the highest international levels of excellence.

www.cambridge.org
Information on this title: www.cambridge.org/9781108959186

© Cambridge University Press 2021

First published 2021

20 19 18 17 16 15 14 13 12 11 10 9 8 7 6 5 4 3

Printed in Great Britain by CPI Group (UK) Ltd, Croydon CR0 4YY

A catalogue record for this publication is available from the British Library

ISBN 978-1-108-95918-6 Paperback
ISBN 978-1-108-95921-6 eBook

Contents

Acknowledgements and Thanks

The authors and publishers acknowledge the following sources of copyright material and are grateful for the permissions granted. While every effort has been made, it has not always been possible to identify the sources of all the material used, or to trace all copyright holders. If any omissions are brought to our notice, we will be happy to include the appropriate acknowledgements on reprinting and in the next update to the digital edition, as applicable.

Text

Quote from research study, Linguistics and English Language by Isabelle Buchstaller, http://www.lel.ed.ac.uk/. Reproduced with kind permission of Isabelle Buchstaller; Quote from Quotatives: new trends and sociolinguistic implications, Isabelle Buchstaller, 01.01.2014. Republished with permission of John Wiley & Sons Books, permission conveyed through Copyright Clearance Center, Inc.

URL

The publisher has used its best endeavors to ensure that the URLs for external websites referred to in this book are correct and active at the time of going to press. However, the publisher has no responsibility for the websites and can make no guarantee that a site will remain live or that the content is or will remain appropriate.

Thanks

Warm thanks to series editor Scott Thornbury for his wise and generous feedback as this book grew from initial concept to completion, to the publishing team at Cambridge University Press – Jo Timerick, Karen Momber and Alison Sharpe – for their sympathetic ELT advice and meticulous copy-editing, and of course to the many teachers and students who asked me these questions in the first place.

Why I wrote this book

There comes a point, in the lives of language learners, when they become aware of two Great Truths. The language they're learning is changing, even while they're learning it. And the version of the language they're being taught isn't the only one. Sooner or later, everyone has to come to terms with *language change* and *language variation*. All languages change and vary. The only ones that don't are dead.

It shouldn't really be a surprise. After all, the learners' own mother-tongues change and vary too. But an unexpected encounter with a usage they've not been taught can be disconcerting. In the case of English, the changes and variations in usage are especially noticeable, due to its long and complex social and political history, as are the irregularities that have developed as a result. And one of the commonest questions teachers get asked, especially by young learners, is: Why?

Knowing the answers can be really helpful. It does more than satisfy a curiosity. It can increase learners' confidence, as they come to appreciate that the variation they've noticed isn't random, but reflects principles and practices that they can empathize with, for these operate in their mother-tongue too. And knowing why a usage has developed in English can help them consolidate it in their production and better appreciate it in their comprehension.

In this book I give my answers to some of the questions I've been asked about usage variation and change in English. While most of the questions begin with a specific example raised by the enquirer, the explanation usually leads to a number of related usages, and some general issues emerge as a result. The history of the language, and its literature, is a recurring theme.

I've grouped the questions into five broad areas – Words and Idioms, Grammar, Pronunciation, Spelling and Punctuation, and Genres – though of course there are numerous points of overlap.

Further reading on many of the topics in this book can be found in my *Cambridge Encyclopedia of the English Language* (3rd edition, 2020). For the history of individual words, the online *Oxford English Dictionary* (oed.com) is an invaluable source. All the main corpora on English can be found, with convenient links, at the English Corpora website created by Mark Davies: www.english-corpora.org

A: Words and idioms

This section contains topics that at first sight seem very specific, but they raise general issues about the nature of change and variation that apply throughout the lexicon. I begin with the three questions most often asked about the general character of English vocabulary.

---

1 How many words are there in the English Language?

2 How many new words come into English every year?

3 Why is English vocabulary so varied?

4 Why do I hear two forms used in a sentence like *Talk among(st) yourselves*?

5 What's the difference between *a cup* and *a mug*?

6 Why do people say *phonetic* and *grammatical* and not *phonetical* and *grammatic*?

7 I hear people adding *-ish* to words a lot. What does it mean?

8 What should we call the meal in the middle of the day: *lunch* or *dinner*?

9 Why is everyone these days saying *you're welcome* in response to thanks?

10 What does it mean when someone adds *at all* at the end of a question?

11 Why do English speakers sometimes use pidgin English, as in *long time no see*?

12 Is it all right to say *she looks well in a black dress* rather than *looks good*?

13 Why do people say the same thing twice, as in *it takes what it takes*?

14 What is happening in new expressions like *well good*?

---

1 | How many words are there in the English Language?

And, even more intriguing, how many do you know?

The first question is easy to answer: nobody knows. You might think all we have to do is count the words in the biggest dictionaries. The *Oxford English Dictionary*, for example, has over 600,000 entries. But there are lots of words that this or any other dictionary wouldn't include.

Even if we restrict our count to words in Standard English, the biggest dictionaries could never keep up with the idiosyncratic usages that we see all around us. Compound words are especially difficult to handle. In a newspaper article on the health value of red wine, I find *best-scoring grape*, *a mould-prone climate*, *barrel-ageing* and *bottle-ageing*. The writer talks about *heart-friendly* wines, supporting the *red-wine-is-best* theory. These are all clearly intelligible words, and some are going to be encountered quite often. *Heart-friendly*, for example, had 270,000 hits on a Google search engine last time I looked. But they are not going to be included in a dictionary because their meaning is obvious from their constituent elements.

The vocabulary of science and technology presents another problem. There are, apparently, some million insects already identified, with several million more awaiting description. This means there must be at least a corresponding number of lexical designations enabling English-speaking entomologists to talk about their subject. And similarly, unknown numbers would be found whatever knowledge area we looked at, as academics are always innovating conceptually and devising new terms, or new senses of old terms, to express their fresh thinking.

Then there's slang. By its nature slang changes rapidly and is difficult to track. Few of the dozens of words for being drunk, for example, will appear in a dictionary – *lagered*, *boxed*, *treed*, *bladdered* ... – and of course nobody can be sure whether any of these items are still in use.

Above all there's the problem of capturing new words that arise as a result of English becoming a global language. Most of the adaptation that takes place when a 'new English' emerges is in vocabulary, as speakers adapt the language to meet their communicative needs. We need only think of a country's fauna and flora, food and drink, mythology and religion, oral and written literature, local laws and customs, leisure and the arts, social structure ... . So, when a community adopts English, and starts to use it in relation to all areas of life, there's inevitably going to be a great deal of lexical creation. To take just one example, there are some 20,000 entries in the *Dictionary of Caribbean English* (1996).

What about the second question: how many words do educated native-speakers know – their *passive vocabulary*? How many do *you* know? A difficult question, but one that can be researched. All you have to do is go through a desk dictionary and tick the words you know! More realistically, take a sample of pages and make an estimate. I've done this many times with native-speakers, and the total is usually between forty and fifty thousand, and often twice this number. That may seem a lot, but remember it includes word families, such as *happy, happiness, happily, happy-go-lucky* ... . The total builds up quite quickly. I've also done it with fluent second-language learners, and – surprise? – the figures also approach 40,000+, especially if the learner is an avid reader of English literature and is online a lot. We know more than we think we know.

Active vocabulary is much more difficult to count, as it varies so much from one time and situation to another. (Think of all the words we use at a festival, that are never used at other times of the year.) It includes the words we write as well as speak. Estimates suggest that our active vocabulary is about a third lower than our passive vocabulary. That's still more than most people think. Vocabulary sizes always tend to be underestimated.

Allsopp, R. (1996) *Dictionary of Caribbean English*. Oxford: Oxford University Press.

How many new words come into English every year?

Vocabulary change means two things: the loss of old words and senses and the arrival of new ones. It's difficult to arrive at any accurate figure. We never know which of the new words we hear around us are going to be permanent features of English, and which are transient – the slang and fashionable usage of the moment. A study of the new words and phrases used in English during the 1970s suggests that as many as 75 percent of them ceased to be used after quite a short period of time.

Collections of 'new words' made by various publishers and dictionary-providers, based on words which have been seen in print, indicate that hundreds of new expressions appear each year. For example, the Oxford University Press publication, *Twentieth Century Words*, contains a selection of about 5,000 items such as:

- from the 1990s: applet, Blairism, cool Britannia, Dianamania, docusoap
- from the 1980s: AIDS, backslash, bog-standard, cellphone, designer drug
- from the 1970s: action replay, Betamax, cashpoint, club class, detox.

The average is 500 items a decade – roughly one a week – and this is only a *selection* from everyday written language. The *Longman Guardian Original Selection of New Words* collected words which had come to prominence in written English in 1986: it contained around a thousand. No one has yet devised a technique for capturing the neologisms that enter the spoken language, and which are rarely (sometimes never) written down. And it's even more difficult to capture new meanings of old words, as when *text* and *tweet* developed online uses.

That there should be so many new words entering the language should come as no surprise when we consider the many walks of life which motivate them, such as the arts, business, computing, the environment, leisure, medicine, politics, popular culture, sports, science and technology. In early 2020, for example, words and phrases listed in the Cambridge Dictionary's 'New Words' website included:

- *fearware* – a cyber attack that exploits an existing sense of fear
- *xenobot* – a very small robot created from living cells
- *blue mind* – a calm state of mind caused by being close to water.

Plainly, the array of new words reflects the trends, inventions and attitudes seen in contemporary society. But this raises an interesting question: how do we define 'contemporary society', from the viewpoint of vocabulary change? During the 1980s, it's safe to say that virtually all the new vocabulary people heard in Britain – whether generated within Britain or introduced from elsewhere (e.g. the USA) – would have come from British sources – newspapers, magazines, radio, television, or the local worlds of occupational idiom and street slang. But since the arrival of the internet in its various manifestations, it is now possible for anyone (who has the electronic means) to directly encounter English in its worldwide lexical variety. A decade ago, it would have been extremely difficult for me to have explored the extensive regional vocabulary of, say, South Africa, without actually going to the place. Now it's just a mouse-click away.

The cumulative impact of global English vocabulary is already very noticeable on the internet and must eventually make an impact on our linguistic consciousness, wherever we live. Our comprehension of foreign vocabulary will grow, and in due course some items will enter our spoken or written production. It is not, after all, an entirely passive situation. The millions of (predominantly younger) Britons who now routinely enter chatrooms, write or respond to blogs, play virtual-reality games, and actively participate in social media are encountering an unprecedented range of varieties of English. In just one chatroom there may be participants from any part of the English-speaking world. Different dialects of English become neighbours on the same screen, as do different levels of competence in the use of English. As a result, accommodation will be widespread – and operate in any direction. British people may be influenced by South African English – and of course vice versa. It will be a brave new lexical world.

Ayto, J. (1999) *Twentieth Century Words*. Oxford: Oxford University Press.

Mort, S. (Ed.) (1986) *Longman Guardian Original Selection of New Words*. London: Longman Higher Education.

Why is English vocabulary so varied?

> When people ask this question, they're usually thinking of
> pairs or groups of words such as *royal* and *regal*. Why do
> we have both, when the meaning seems to be the same?

Lexical choices like these reflect the colourful political and cultural
history of the English-speaking peoples over the centuries. My favourite
metaphor is to describe English as a linguistic vacuum-cleaner of a
language, whose users suck in words from other languages whenever
they encounter them. And because of the way English has travelled
the world, several hundred languages have contributed to its lexical
character. Although it began as a Germanic language, some 80 percent
of English vocabulary isn't Germanic at all.

But English was never a purely Germanic language. On the mainland of
Europe, the Germanic languages had already incorporated words from
Latin, and these arrived in Britain with the Anglo-Saxons. Latin then
continued to be an important influence, introducing everyday words to
do with plants and animals, food and drink, buildings, household objects
and many other domains – *butter, mile, wall, street, cat, wine* ... . This
vocabulary continued to expand, with the growing influence of missionary
activity reflected in an increase in words to do with religion and learning.
The Celts lived in Britain before the Anglo-Saxons arrived, and Old English
also contains a few Celtic words, such as *crag* and *brock* (a badger).

The Vikings attacked Britain in the 780s, and an area of eastern
England was for a while subject to Danish laws. A few Old Norse
words are found in Old English writings, but the vast majority aren't
seen until the 13th century. Middle English literature shows hundreds of
Norse loanwords, such as *take, get* and *egg*.

But the Latin and Norse elements in early English are small compared
with the huge impact of French in the Middle Ages – the result of
French power in England after 1066 and of French cultural
pre-eminence in mainland Europe. Anglo-Saxon words couldn't cope

with the new domains of expression introduced by the Normans, such as in law, architecture, music and literature. The new words usually replaced the old ones, but the old words often survived, sometimes developing a different meaning or stylistic use.

Then came the Renaissance, with a massive influence of vocabulary from Latin and Greek. And this is what led to the 'doublets' illustrated by *royal* and *regal*. In Old English, the only way of describing a king would have been *kingly*. Now we find *royal* from French and *regal* from Latin. Similarly, we find such 'triplets' as Old English *ask* supplemented by French *question* and Latin *interrogate*, and Old English *fire* supplemented by French *flame* and Latin *conflagration*. The Latin words look and sound more scholarly or specialized, especially by comparison with the down-to-earth feel of the Anglo-Saxon words. The French words often add an aristocratic tone, as with Old English *clothes* and French *attire*, or Old English *house* and French *mansion*.

An interesting development was when two words with different origins came together into a single idiom. So today we say that something is *fit and proper* or has gone to *wrack and ruin* (combinations of Old English and French). If we want some *peace and quiet* we are joining a French and a Latin word. This is very common in the English used in law, in such pairings as *null and void*, and the well known *to have and to hold* (in the marriage ceremony) and *last will and testament*.

All these lexical options are especially exploited in English literature. Shakespeare couldn't have created the range of his characters without them. But they will be found in everyday English too, especially when we switch between formal and informal styles. And it's rarely possible to substitute one for the other: a *royal residence* belongs to the Queen or a member of her family; a *regal residence* (that is, a magnificent or stately one) could belong to anybody.

4 Why do I hear two forms used in a sentence like *Talk among(st) yourselves?*

> A remarkable range of factors influences our usage.

This is where exploring a corpus is essential, to supplement our poor intuitions. There's certainly a regional difference. In the Corpus of Contemporary American English, I found only 2,405 instances of *amongst* compared to 144,461 instances of *among* – 1.66 percent. In the British National Corpus there were 4,449 instances compared to 22,385 of *among* – 20 percent. But *among* is still overwhelmingly the norm wherever you go.

Where did the *-st* ending come from? It was originally a development of the Old English inflectional ending: *among* + genitive *-es*. We can see an echo of that old ending still in *besides*. Then, in the 16th century, people evidently felt this was related to the *-est* superlative form, as gradually we find the *-st* ending used. We see it also in *against*, where it's the standard form, and in *amidst* (v *amid*) and *whilst* (v *while*), where usage varies. There's also a less used *unbeknownst*, meaning 'unknown', which began as a dialect form and crept into more general use. 'I often am sitting in the rocking-chair unbeknownst to you,' wrote Mrs Gaskell in 1848. A related form, *unknownst*, found mainly in Irish English (as in *unknownst to you*), remained regional.

Is there any difference in meaning? Every modern sense of *among* has a parallel use of *amongst*, as in these examples:

- in relation to local surroundings: *The water rushed among(st) the stones.*
- in relation to a surrounding group: *I stood among(st) the crowd.*
- in relation to a non-surrounding group: *It's popular among(st) my friends.*
- in relation to a particular class: *She is one among(st) many writers who …*
- in relation to division: *We have five pounds among(st) us.*

The only hint of a semantic difference is suggested by the *Oxford English Dictionary* in its entry on *amongst*, describing a nuance not found in *among*: 'generally implying dispersion, intermixture, or shifting position'. So, *I walked amongst the crowd* would suggest a rather more active moving about than *I walked among the crowd*. This would predict that *talk amongst yourselves* would be more frequent than *talk among yourselves* – and indeed it is (seven times more in a Google search).

Perhaps usage is influenced by pronunciation? *Amongst, amidst* and *whilst* all close with a three-element consonant cluster. In colloquial speech, if a consonant begins the following word, as in *amongst people*, the /t/ would usually be dropped. This wouldn't be noticed in informal settings, but it would if, say, a BBC newsreader were to drop it. Speakers on formal occasions would thus be *more* likely to articulate *-st* words carefully, which would promote an association with formality.

The variation in Standard English seems to be chiefly stylistically conditioned: some people just like the sound of *-st* words; others don't. There's also a chronological factor: the *-st* forms are commoner in older texts and among older people. And there's a great deal of regional dialect variation too. But the reasons people give for their like/dislike are conflicting. Some sense its association with regional dialect and feel it's colloquial – 'It sounds northern,' said one person from the south of England. Others find it formal – 'It sounds posh,' said someone from the north who claimed he didn't use *-st* forms at all.

Situations like this soon lead to feelings of uncertainty about what is 'correct'. Long-standing practice might then be changed. I can't otherwise explain why the traditional usage we see in signs, such as *Shoes repaired while you wait* should have been altered to *Shoes repaired whilst you wait*. Fashion soon removes such feelings, though, and today I see *whilst you wait* signs all over the place. But when I typed that string into a Google search engine I was asked 'Did you mean *while you wait*?' So it's not there yet.

What's the difference between *a cup* and *a mug*?

The way in which these two words interact was a topic of national interest in 2015, explored by 25 regional radio stations across the UK.

This is a perfect example of the way words interact and change their meaning as a result of regional, social and cultural factors. Exploring the history behind semantically related words is always fascinating.

In the beginning, there was only the cup. The Anglo-Saxon word was *cuppe*, borrowed from Latin *cuppa*, meaning simply a drinking-vessel. The form of the vessel then developed in two directions: without a stem (as in the modern *teacup*) and with a stem and foot (as in a *wine-cup*), reflecting a diversity of functions. It had a strong religious connotation in Christianity, used in the sense of 'chalice' in a 14th-century translation of the Bible and thus into modern usage (as in *communion cup*). In the 17th century, it also developed an ornamental sense, naming a prize in a contest, which is the commonest modern application. Colloquially, it became a replacement for the liquid a cup might contain, as in *cuppa* ('cup of tea'), and that in turn led to idioms, as in *That's not my cup of tea* ('not something I like').

The history of *mug* is totally different, arriving in the Middle Ages. It may be an adaptation of a Latin word for a measuring vessel (*modius*). From the outset it seemed to refer more to the physical object than to the content it might contain. It comes to be used with such adjectives as *large* and *half-pint*, and with words that describe its material, such as *silver* or *stone*. We also often find it used in relation to a location – a steaming mug of tea might be left *on the bench*, *by the fire* … . Cups weren't so often 'located' in this way.

The early use of *mug* was mainly in regional dialects, and especially in Scotland, for any earthenware bowl or pot. It began to be used routinely for a drinking vessel in the 17th century, and gradually came to be distinguished from the tapering cup by its cylindrical shape and larger size. But it was the social activity that led to the main difference between the two.

In the 18th century, the taking of tea became a mark of high society. The word *teacup* arrived. Saucers joined cups as the norm (to ensure that any spillage was contained). Mugs then became associated with lower-class activities, where spilling didn't matter so much, and where the larger size reflected the thirstiness of the drinker. Early examples of *mug* are almost all to do with beer. Mugs of tea were drunk by people who were either blue-collar workers or – later – those who wanted to be thought of as down-to-earth, ordinary types. These connotations remain today.

As the taking of tea became less class-conscious, and a more informal occasion, it led to the shortened form *cuppa* in British regional English. There seems to have been a need to get away from the formality of 'high tea'. By contrast, there is no word *mugga* – presumably because *mug* was always felt to be associated with less formal settings.

The usage of the two words now differs greatly, reflecting their different social history. When people talk of *cups*, they're more likely to be thinking of the contents rather than the object. We *sip* and *pour* a cup of tea. We talk about a *lovely cup of coffee*, a *perfect cup of tea*. The cup is associated with drinking as a social event: we *offer* someone a cup of coffee, and people *enjoy* a cup of tea together. It also marks the passing of time: we talk about an *early morning cup of tea*, my *third cup of coffee*. Try replacing the word *cup* with *mug* in these examples, and you can sense the difference. *Mug* is actually very rare in these circumstances: in the 650-million-word Bank of English corpus, *cup of tea* is fifteen times more common than *mug of tea*.

6 Why do people say *phonetic* and *grammatical* and not *phonetical* and *grammatic?*

There are dozens of words that illustrate the same usage issue.

In a specialist domain, the only thing you can do is identify and follow majority usage. In linguistics these days it is *phonetic*, *phonological*, *grammatical*, *syntactic* and *semantic* (but you'll find the alternatives in older usage). You can tell the difference between a specialist and a non-specialist by the ending: those who talk about *syntactical structures* or *semantical problems* or *linguistical issues* are not likely to be specialists in linguistics. A usage to beware relates to *dialect*: in linguistics, the adjective is *dialectal*, not *dialectical*, to avoid confusion with the sense in philosophy relating to *dialectic* (logic or reasoning). But with pairs like *alphabetic* and *alphabetical*, *analytic* and *analytical*, or *diacritic* and *diacritical*, there's no difference in meaning.

The issue goes well beyond the terminology of linguistics, as with *mystic(al)*, *poetic(al)*, *ironic(al)*, *rhythmic(al)*, *problematic(al)* ... . Usually there's no difference in meaning, but there may be a stylistic or regional preference. Where the two forms are synonymous, people generally opt for the shorter alternative; but the extra *-al* syllable can sometimes produce a more euphonious utterance, avoiding a clash of consonants or promoting a better rhythm (compare *geographic contours* v *geographical contours*). The shorter form is more likely to be made into a noun, as in *a dialectic, a diacritic, a mystic, a comic.*

Collocations are likely to differ. In the sense of 'powered by electricity', we see *electric* used in the music domain (*electric guitar/keyboard*) and in relation to sensations (*electric shock, the air was electric*). When a broad notion is involved, or a person, we are more likely to see *electrical* (*electrical equipment/wiring experts*). If I ask someone, 'Have you brought your electrical equipment?' I mean all the tools to do with electricity needed to do the job; if I ask, 'Have you brought your electric drill?' I mean a drill operated by electricity (not by some other method).

The *-al* ending usually suggests a broader meaning – more things are *comical* than are *comic*. A comic film is a comedy. A comical film might also be a (failed) tragedy. The sense has developed of 'unintentionally humorous'.

A subject area is also more likely to have *-al*: *electrical engineering*. And similarly, we see *political* (to do with politics) and *historical* (to do with history). Specific meanings have developed for the alternatives: in relation to decisions, *politic* means 'sensible, judicious'; in relation to people, 'prudent, shrewd', or (in a reversal that often causes ambiguity) 'crafty, cunning'. If someone were to call me 'politic', I would have no idea (without a broader context) whether it was a compliment or an insult.

Similarly, *historic* has developed the sense of 'great' (from the point of view of history), as in *historic opportunity/occasion*. This sense emerges especially when used with an intensifier, as in *a very historic place*. The contrast can be seen with writers: a *historical novelist* writes about history; a *historic novelist* would be a famous one. Or, to come back home: a *historical linguist* is a student of the history of language; a *historic linguist* would be a really well-known one.

The general v specific meaning can go the other way. *Economic* tends to be the more general these days (*economic theory/union/policy*), used for the science of economics or the economy in general (*economic geography*) and in compounds (*socio-economic*). *Economic management* is a subject of study; *economical management* is how we save money. *Economical* has also developed in a different direction, being used for abstractions that are nothing to do with money, such as *economical style/explanation* – and, perhaps most famously, in the idiom *to be economical with the truth* (to deliberately misrepresent the facts).

Clearly, it isn't possible to generalize. Each case needs to be examined individually, using an up-to-date dictionary, for in this area of the lexicon, fashions can change quite quickly.

7   I hear people adding *-ish* to words a lot. What does it mean?

> The form has been around much longer than you might think, but we hear some fresh uses today.

The usage does seem to be used in increasingly varied ways. As an adjective suffix it goes back a long way. In the sense of 'somewhat', we find it added to monosyllabic adjectives from Middle English times – colour words such as *bluish* (1398) and *blackish* (1450) are among the earliest. The usage then extended to other monosyllabic adjectives, such as *brightish* (1584), *coldish* (1589) and *goodish* (1751), and has continued to extend over the centuries. Adjectives ending in *-y* and *-w* attract it too, as in *sillyish* (1766) and *narrowish* (1823). In the early 20th century, we find it used for hours of the day or number of years, probably motivated by *earlyish* and *latish* – *See you at eightish, She's thirty-ish.* Note *elevenish, forty-five-ish, 1932-ish,* and so on, where the root has three or more syllables. Also note that the sense of approximation can be colloquially reinforced by other words of similar meaning: *I'll be with you about sevenish more or less.* That speaker is being really vague!

There's a second use of *-ish*, where it's added to nouns in the sense of 'having the character of'. Some, such as *childish* and *churlish*, and the nationhood names such as *English* and *Scottish*, go back to Old English. Among later arrivals are *boyish* (1542) and *waggish* (1600) – the latter a first recorded use in Shakespeare, as is *foppish* and *unbookish*. (Shakespeare quite liked the suffix – *knavish, dwarfish, thievish, hellish, wolvish* ...). Most have a derogatory sense. Again, most are monosyllabic, but we do find the occasional longer form, such as *babyish, womanish* and *outlandish*.

This trend really took off in the 19th century, when novelists and journalists extended it to proper names. We find *Queen Annish, Mark Twainish,* and suchlike, as well as some colloquial phrases – *You look very out-of-townish, He has a how-do-you-do-ish manner.* And today we see the further extension of these patterns in informal contexts to longer adjectives. We add *-ish* now to just about every adjective under the sun, such as *beautifulish, Europeanish, freezingish, exhaustedish* ... . I can't see any restriction here, other than stylistic – they are informal, colloquial, jocular, daring. There's a YouTube site called *extraordinaryish*. But one senses the novelty – as does Google. When I typed *-ish* in, to see if it was used (I got 193 hits), the search engine was worried. 'Did you mean extraordinary fish?' it asked me.

The most recent development has been the use of *ish* in its 'somewhat' sense as a separate sentence, in much the same way as we can use *sort of*, *kind of* and *not very*.

A: *Are you interested in going to the show?*
B: *Not very./Sort of./Kind of./Ish.*

Ish there is short for *interestedish*. This kind of usage has been recorded only since the 1980s. Its typical use is as a conversational rejoinder, where the sense of 'in a way, partially' generally gives it the force of a criticism, though often in a jocular or sympathetic way. Intonationally, it usually has a falling-rising tone (of doubt, hesitation).

A: *Robin sang brilliantly last night.*   B: *Ish.*

Someone can add it to what they have just said, acting as a sentence modifier:

I like broccoli. Ish.

The negative meaning comes out even more strongly in the derived form *ishy*. Now it means 'of poor quality':

A: *Did you like the food at the restaurant last night?*
B: *I thought it was a bit ishy.*

But it has a very positive connotation in *Ish*, the title of a book by British artist Peter H. Reynolds (2004), in which a creative spirit learns that a drawing doesn't have to look exactly like anything. As a blurb for the book said at the time: 'thinking "*ish*-ly" is far more wonderful than "getting it right".'

8 What should we call the meal in the middle of the day: *lunch* or *dinner*?

People have been debating this question for over 100 years, and the arguments still continue.

This is a good example of how usage and culture interact. Originally, there was only *dinner* – a word that arrived from French in the 13th century for the chief meal of the day, usually eaten around midday. In Shakespeare's *As You Like It* (4.1.166), Orlando tells Rosalind he has to leave her for two hours, 'I must attend the Duke at dinner. By two o'clock I will be with thee again.'

The words *luncheon* and *lunch* both arrived in the late 16th century, though not in their modern sense. A *lunch(eon)* was a thick piece of food – a hunk of something. People would talk about a *luncheon of cheese* or a *lunch of bacon*. In the 17th century, it was a light repast taken between the main meals. The modern use of *lunch* isn't recorded until 1829, and not everyone liked it, but it was eventually adopted by high society. At the same time, *luncheon* was attracting criticism as a word unsuitable for use in those circles. But *dinner* was also being frowned upon, because of its growing lower-class associations. There was a great deal of social confusion.

Today, dictionaries define *dinner* as a main meal, and leave open the question of time of day. This is because there's still a great deal of regional and social class variation. In many parts of the UK (and also in several other English-speaking countries), when people take their main meal in the middle of the day it's called *dinner*. They wouldn't use the word *lunch* at all; and for them an evening meal would be *tea* or more likely *supper*. But for 'the professional and fashionable classes' (as the *Oxford English Dictionary* elegantly puts it), *dinner* is the evening meal, and *lunch* is what is eaten in the middle of the day.

In Britain, this issue was highlighted in the 1950s when a great deal of publicity was given to the suggestion that upper-class (or 'U') speakers said *lunch* or *luncheon*; everyone else ('non-U') said *dinner*.

The situation was never as neat and tidy as the distinction suggested. U-speakers certainly called their midday meal *lunch(eon)*, but if they had a dog they would give it *dinner* at that time of day. And businessmen having an evening meal in a restaurant might pay for it with *luncheon-vouchers*.

For many nowadays, *lunch* is a light meal – it might only be a sandwich – and several expressions have evolved to capture the possible lunchtime variations, such as *light lunch*, *heavy lunch*, *liquid lunch* (consisting chiefly of alcohol), *picnic lunch*, *Sunday lunch* and *working lunch*. These don't apply to the word *dinner*, which still retains its traditional associations. People have a *candlelit dinner* or a *romantic dinner*. And, behaviour being what it is, we often hear of a *TV dinner* (eaten while watching the television). *Luncheon* had a peak of usage around the 1920s, but now seems to be disappearing apart from in very formal social contexts.

As always, there are exceptions. In schools, the traditional phrase for the lunchtime meal is *school dinners,* and the people who serve it are *dinner ladies*. Children bring in their *dinner money*. And when chef Jamie Oliver started his campaign on British television in 2005 for more nutritious food in school lunches, he called it *Jamie's School Dinners*. However, usage changes. Children often now take a *packed lunch* to school in a *lunchbox*, never a *packed dinner* in a *dinner-box*, and they might pay *lunch money*.

Another illustration of change is on Christmas day, when many of the families who celebrate that feast sit down to a *Christmas dinner* – in the early afternoon. I increasingly hear *Christmas lunch* for the festival – something that's entirely normal in Australia, and common in New Zealand and South Africa, too. But if we look at the large collections of data (corpora), we find *Christmas dinner* is many times more frequent in most parts of the English-speaking world.

Why is everyone these days saying *you're welcome* in response to thanks?

It's not only 'these days', as Shakespeare and other writers show us.

Certainly the usage is very frequent today around the English-speaking world – and in the English text-messaging world, where *yw* is a widely used abbreviation. It seems to have become the expression of choice in service environments (such as responding to customers who say *thank you* in a restaurant), and it has been seized (I suspect with some relief) as an easy polite response by service personnel who have English as a second language. It isn't the only option: expressions such as *no worries* (e.g. in Australia) and *no problem* are also widely heard, as is *sure*, though these are more colloquial.

The analysis of thanks and its consequences is a popular topic within the field of pragmatics (a field that studies the choices people make when they use language in different situations, the reasons for those choices, and the effects they convey). It always interests language learners to note the differences between English and the way their mother tongue handles acknowledgement – German *bitte*, Italian *prego*, and suchlike. But to fully understand the modern usage we need a historical perspective.

You're welcome turns out not to be a recent development. You can find examples dating from the mid-1850s, as in Charles Dickens' *Little Dorrit*, Chapter 2:

> 'I thank you,' said the other, 'very heartily for your confidence.' 'Don't mention it,' returned Mr Meagles, 'I am sure you are quite welcome.'

This is a polite response to a prior expression of gratitude. It's a usage that has developed naturally from the earlier greeting, as when someone says 'You are welcome,' to a visitor. This has been in English for hundreds of years. Here's an example from Shakespeare's *The Taming of the Shrew* (4.2.72):

> Pedant: God save you, sir.
> Tranio: And you sir. You are welcome.

It's a very short step from here to the acknowledgement usage.

It's difficult to say when the modern usage took over. There would have been a transitional period in which people would have reacted uncertainly to it. I've been looking for examples, and think I may have found one. What do you make of this, from Thackeray's *The Wolves and the Lamb*, Act 1, written at the same time as *Little Dorrit*?

> MRS. PRIOR. Oh, how thoughtful it was of your ladyship to ask me to stay to tea!
> LADY K. With your daughter and the children? Indeed, my good Mrs. Prior, you are very welcome!
> MRS. PRIOR. Ah! but isn't it a cause of thankfulness to be MADE welcome.

Is Lady K's response to Mrs Prior a politeness formula, or a literal welcoming? My feeling is that it is the former, and this prompts Mrs Prior to focus on the latter.

It's a slightly uncomfortable position to be placed in, knowing you have to thank someone for being thanked, or to dismiss their thanks as being unnecessary. So it's not surprising to find people opting for other expressions – often slightly awkward, as in *think nothing of it* or *not at all*. Some are predictable; others not. A predictable development was the use of *pleasure* in the context of a polite exchange. The first known usage in literature is by Charles Dickens in *The Pickwick Papers*, Chapter 2 (1837):

> 'Glass of wine, Sir?' 'With pleasure,' said Mr Pickwick.

It's easy to see how *my pleasure* might then develop as a formal response to thanks. What surprises me is that its first recorded use in the *Oxford English Dictionary* isn't until 1950, over a century later. I would have expected it to be earlier – and maybe one day somebody will find a prior instance.

And an unpredictable development? The use of *no problem* dates from 1950s. But who would ever have guessed that, some 31 years later, people would start adding an *-o* suffix from Spanish and start saying, as a light-hearted and very informal response, *no problemo*.

10 What does it mean when someone adds *at all* at the end of a question?

Several fascinating variations in usage emerge around the English-speaking world.

We need to distinguish two uses of *at all*. In a sentence like *I have no problem at all*, it's postmodifying *problem*, and simply adding emphasis to the negative phrase. There's a similar effect when someone responds to a question with *not at all*. The extra emphasis makes the denial sound more polite or sincere compared with the abruptness of a single *no*. Compare:

Do you mind if I move this chair?   No.
Do you mind if I move this chair?   Not at all.

The meaning of *at all* here is 'in any way', 'in the least', 'to any degree'.

There was an earlier use in affirmative sentences too, dating from the 14th century, with a positive meaning: 'in every way', 'altogether', as in *It's the greatest fun at all* (i.e. 'it's certainly the greatest fun'). This is still heard today in some regional dialects, especially in Ireland, the Caribbean, and parts of the USA, but it never survived in Standard English.

The second use is when *at all* occurs at the end of a question and refers back to the entire sentence, not just to the immediately preceding word. This is the use illustrated by *Did you go there at all?* and in these examples: *Why should we believe that at all? How can Mike write such a letter at all?*

This use is also quite old, with instances recorded since the 16th century. It functions here much like a sentence particle or tag, such as *indeed* or *huh*, but with a more specific meaning. From a pragmatic point of view, it softens the force of the question. In some contexts the best way of glossing it would be 'may I ask?', as in *How's your mother at all?* In others the meaning would be more like 'would you say?' This is the sense we need when we encounter it in one of James Joyce's stories in *Dubliners*. One of the characters asks about Father Keon: *Is he a priest at all?* In cases like these, we might hear reduplication, adding extra emphasis: *Is he a priest at all at all?* We may even hear triples. I had an aunt in County Wexford who said things like, *Will you be after going there at all at all at all?*

In a negative context, sentence-modifying *at all* is even older, with the earliest recorded instance being in 1476. Shakespeare was fond of it, using it over sixty times in the plays, as in this instance from *A Midsummer Night's Dream* (5.1.198): 'I kiss the wall's hole, not your lips at all.' The *at all* doesn't just refer to the lips, but modifies *kiss*, as can be seen if the sentence is expanded and the position changed: 'I kiss the wall's hole, and I do not at all kiss your lips.'

I mentioned an Irish connection. Sentence-modifying *at all* was always strong in Ireland, and would eventually arrive from there into the USA, Canada and the Caribbean. Richard Allsopp calls it 'an Irish importation' in his *Dictionary of Caribbean English* (1996) and gives several examples of its emphatic use in questions and conditionals:

> If you bother me at all at all today, you go nowhere (Trinidad)
> You ent [haven't] see 'im at all at all at all (Guyana)

All this reminds me of an Irish joke. An American tourist arrives in Dublin and asks a local: 'What's the difference between a single yellow line and a double yellow line?' The Irishman replies: 'The single yellow line means "no parking at all"; the double yellow line means "no parking at all, at all".'

Why did this question get raised at all? There has probably been an increase in spoken frequency which is making sharp-eared learners notice it. But I haven't noticed an increase at all in written English yet.

Allsopp, R. (1996) *Dictionary of Caribbean English*. Oxford: Oxford University Press.

Why do English speakers sometimes use pidgin English, as in *long time no see?*

Cinema has had a lot to do with the history of this usage, but there's more to it than the label 'pidgin' suggests.

Nobody knows exactly what the origin is of this expression, meaning 'It's a long time since I've seen you'. The earliest reference in the *Oxford English Dictionary* is 1900, the context indicating a simplified English being used in conversation with Native Americans. It probably caught on through cowboy movies. Certainly it was in US usage long before it arrived in British English. But the same pidgin expression has been noted in several other contact situations around the world, so it may have multiple origins.

It's rare to find pidginized expressions becoming part of Standard English idiom, but it's not alone. There's the analogous *long time no hear*, and I can imagine that any verb of communication could be used within this frame, such as *speak* or *talk*. Indeed, any verb referring to an action that hasn't taken place for a long time could be used in it, but the context would usually be jocular, as in *long time no see sun*.

Then there's the fictitious *me Tarzan, you Jane* – 'fictitious' because it doesn't actually turn up in the Tarzan books – another instance of the influence of cinema. And this next one has a proverbial African source: *softly, softly, catchee monkey* (also heard as *slowly, slowly ...*), said when someone is being extremely cautious about carrying out an action or advising someone to be patient to achieve an end. The proverb lives on in the expression *a softly softly approach* to something, and achieved fame when *Softly, Softly* was used as the title of a BBC television police/crime series in the 1960s.

Some of these expressions have a long pedigree. *Dog eat dog* refers to people from the same background harming each other. It goes back to a Latin proverb, *Canis caninem non est* – 'dog does not eat dog' – and is found in English as early as the 16th century. As an adjective, it's common in business and political circles: a *dog-eat-dog world* is a ruthlessly competitive one. *No can do* is more recent: a 19th-century borrowing from Chinese pidgin English, meaning both 'it can't be done' or 'I can't do it'.

How unusual are these constructions? They're not so far away from the traditional two-part elliptical constructions often heard in proverbial utterances, and still being created today. Most are self-explanatory:

the more, the merrier
once bitten, twice shy
out of sight, out of mind
more haste, less speed
like father, like son
first come, first served
here today, gone tomorrow
waste not, want not
no pain, no gain
garbage in, garbage out (in digital contexts)

Nor are they far away from those colloquial expressions where the impact relies greatly on ellipsis, such as *24-7* ('always available, 24 hours a day, seven days a week'), first recorded in the 1980s. Also popular since the 1980s is *been there, done that* – said when reacting to a remark or situation that we find totally familiar. It may express a reinforcing friendly empathy – 'yes, I've done that too' – or a negative attitude, showing lack of interest, or even boredom, though in a flippant kind of way. The implication is: 'no need to have said that'. Derived forms can be heard too, such as *been there, seen that* – and if we really want to be emphatic: *been there, seen that, done that, got the T-shirt.*

Is it all right to say *she looks well in a black dress* rather than *looks good?*

To answer this, we need to consider differences of meaning, grammatical factors and prescriptive views about usage.

This uncertainty probably comes from being taught that *to look well* is to appear healthy whereas *to look good* is to be attractive. The distinction isn't so clear-cut. These days *good* can be used in the health context, and *well* has a long history of use in relation to appearance.

I'll take *good* first. In the early 20th century, *look good* and *listen good* emerged in American English in the sense of 'look/sound promising'. There's a first recorded usage of 1914. This developed into a general sense of *good* to mean 'in a satisfactory frame of mind', 'coping well with life', and suchlike. It's most often heard these days in response to a *How are you?* type of question. *I'm well* means 'I'm well in health'. *I'm good* means 'things are OK for me right now'. It's a new and very useful semantic distinction in English. However, it's colloquial, youthful, and originally American, so many older people, especially in Britain, don't like it.

The use of *well* in relation to appearance isn't new. In 1687, Jean de Thévenot describes the horses of the Grand Signior's militia in his *Travels into the Levant*: 'the Stirrops [stirrups] very short, but yet they look very well'. Over a century later, in Jane Austen's *Emma,* Chapter 35 (1815), there's an example relating specifically to clothing: Mrs Elton asks Jane if it would be a good thing to put some fancy trimming onto her dress: 'Do you think it will look well?' The usage continued to be frequent during the Victorian period, with *well* often modified by *very*, but by the mid-20th-century it was beginning to sound old-fashioned. The *Oxford English Dictionary* actually labels the usage 'somewhat archaic'.

So what has made *looks good* come back into use so much today that people are asking questions about it? It may be that the way *good* developed a sense in relation to 'state of mind' has made the expression less likely to be used in relation to appearance. *She looks good* is now potentially ambiguous: does it mean that she is behaving as if in a happy frame of mind, or that she has dressed impressively? And these days there is a third possibility: does it mean she is carrying out an action in a successful way? You'll recognize this last use from such contexts as American space rocket launches: *It's looking good!*

There may also have been a prescriptive reaction against *good*: to modify a verb, in traditional grammar, we are told we need to use an adverb. *Well* is an adverb, but *good* is an adjective. Therefore, *well* is likely to be preferred by people who want to respect the traditional rules, and I expect many learners have simply been told that it's wrong. Also, the fact that there's an American usage around will reinforce the antagonism to *good* in the minds of some British speakers.

It's difficult to use the big corpora to clarify the situation, as general counts tell us nothing about the senses involved. *Look* and its variants (*looks*, *looking*, *looked*) followed by *good* is still several times more frequent than followed by *well*, and it would take a lengthy piece of research to distinguish the citations that display the sense of appearance from those that display other senses. If there's a modern trend towards using such sentences as *She looks well in a black dress*, it must be very recent.

But, caution: there are some situations in which sentences like *You look well* (in relation to appearance) are not interpreted in a positive way, such as (according to a lengthy controversy in 2019 on the Mumsnet website) after just having had a baby. For some, *she's looking well* is a euphemistic way of saying 'she looks fat'. For them, *well* is out; and *good* is not very strong. So is there anything else they can say to express a real compliment? Yes. *Great.*

13 | Why do people say the same thing twice, as in *it takes what it takes?*

Isn't this a tautology? Yes, but a surprisingly useful one.

Tautology is usually thought of as something to be avoided, as when someone talks about *a necessary requirement* or *a sad misfortune*. Prescriptive guides to English style always condemn it. But there are occasions when saying the same thing twice actually has a purpose. We need to 'state the obvious', and in so doing, say something that isn't obvious at all. If I return from a restaurant, and somebody asks me what the food was like, and I say, 'You get what you get,' that is saying more than what the words suggest. The food was pretty ordinary, or worse.

There are dozens of cases like this, and *it takes what it takes* is one of them. You always have to put such expressions in context to see what they mean. Here, I might be doing a job and someone asks me how long it will take or how much effort I'm prepared to put into it. I've no idea. So I say, 'It takes what it takes.' A book by Trevor Moawad, a mental conditioning coach, is actually called *It Takes What It Takes* (2020) – all about how to deal with even the most challenging circumstances.

Here are some more examples:

- *It's as long as it's long.*
- *A man's gotta do what a man's gotta do.*
- *I'll be ready when I'm ready (and not before)!*
- *It is what it is.*
- *Some things are difficult because they're difficult.*
- *Whatever will be, will be.*
- *Boys will be boys.*
- *Enough is enough.*
- *A deal is a deal.*
- *You two will never agree – he's him and you're you.*
- *A large work is difficult because it is large.*

This last one is from the Preface to Samuel Johnson's enormous *Dictionary of the English Language* (1755).

Sometimes an author adds a helpful gloss to say what is meant. In *A Hero of our Time*, Chapter 18 (1840) Mikhail Lermontov has his character say, 'If I die, then I die! The loss to the world won't be great'.

Why do we say such things? The sentences can be interpreted in various ways, depending on the context. The usual intention is to halt a dialogue – an avoidance strategy: the speaker doesn't want to go into any further detail; there's no more to be said. They could be an assertive strategy: 'Don't ask me pointless questions when I've got a job to do'. They could be a prompt, offering the listener the opportunity to pick up the conversational 'ball'. And there are other pragmatic possibilities. A lot depends on the tone of voice in which the words are said, and the accompanying facial expression.

We learn the value of tautology at an early age. Children encounter it all the time.

> *Why is it time for bed, mummy? Because it's time for bed.*

And it's common in storytelling, where the tautology adds dramatic emphasis.

> *The beanstalk was as big as big could be.*
> *The snow was as white as white as only snow can be.*

A review of a mobile phone says: *A 4.3-inch handset is about as small as small gets these days.* An ad for a really expensive holiday hotel in the Caribbean concludes: *This is as exclusive as exclusive gets.* Even scientists do it. In a physics textbook, after describing the size of the smallest known particle, the writer ends with: *That's really small – as small as small gets.*

What is happening in new expressions like *well good*?

This is another case where the usage has a long history, even though some modern trends are taking it in new directions.

This is an intensifying use of *well* used with adjectives: it means 'very very', 'absolutely', 'thoroughly'. But it isn't new. The *Oxford English Dictionary* has examples that go back as far as Old English, such as *well sharp* and *well tame*. And what do we find in the 13th century? Robert of Gloucester describing England as 'a wel god lond' – a very good land. Later uses include *well able*, *well old*, *well long* and *well happy*. There are even instances of *well* being used with comparatives, such as *well better* and *well faster*.

The usage has never disappeared, as these modern examples show:

I found the visit well worthwhile.
By ten, the dancers were all well tired.
Wait until the paint is well dry.
Make sure the valve is well open.

Well seems to be especially comfortable before the set of words beginning with *a-* which fall midway between adjectives and adverbs, and which are usually used after the verb:

The children are well asleep.
I'm well awake.
I'm well aware of the consequences.

This last example shows how *well*-phrases are often followed by some sort of postmodification:

I'm well capable of doing that.
We're well familiar with the motorway route.
They're well willing to help.

Using *well*-phrases in attributive position is possible but less usual. Here are two examples from the Web:

The arguments are taking a well-familiar path.
We are seeking a well-suitable person to fill the position of ...

An interesting point of pronunciation is that the primary stress is very commonly placed on *well*, not on the adjective. This is especially the case when an expression goes before the noun.

So is there anything new at all about the type of construction heard in *well good*? Since the 1970s, there's been a noticeable increase in adjectives expressing personal emotions or attitudes:

> *I'm well happy.*
> *Chelsea were well lucky to win that match.*
> *I was well excited to see the dolphins.*
> *We're all well proud of you.*

Expressions of this kind are especially common in British English – the *Oxford English Dictionary* actually labels them as 'British slang' – but corpus studies show their use in Ireland, Australia, New Zealand and South Africa, and a sprinkling elsewhere. The citations also show that they are much more commonly used for positive emotions, as illustrated above: negative ones, such as *well angry*, *well sad* and *well miserable*, are rare.

What about *well* with the comparative adjective – is this obsolete? Not on social media forums like Facebook, where it can often be seen as a colloquial replacement for *much* or *far*:

> *Green shirts are well better than blue shirts.*
> *You might be paid less but you will be well happier.*

That it's a young person's trend is clear when we encounter older people treating it satirically. I found a 'get-well-soon' card that has on its front page: 'Get well-better soon, innit'. But there may be some regional and occupational factors to add to the mix. It's surprising how often I see Liverpool turning up as a source in the corpus examples, and also sports commentary.

In most cases, the phrases don't work comfortably before a noun. We're not so likely to encounter a *well-happy person* or *a group of well-tired dancers*. But, with English, we should never say never, especially where young people are concerned. Corpus exploration – or a simple Google search – will usually present us with an example to puncture any complacency. I've just discovered a Scottish group of musicians who call themselves The Well Happy Band.

B: Grammar

Variations in grammatical usage, and especially so many irregular forms, regularly trigger questions from learners. *Why*-questions are the commonest. The explanations take us down diverse paths of meaning, culture and style, all of which help to make the study of grammar come alive.

15 Can *a* be used before an uncountable noun?

16 Why is the article dropped before some nouns, as in *look what baby's doing*?

17 Why do some teachers tell me I shouldn't begin a sentence with *and*?

18 Why do we say *I am, am I* and *I'm not*, but *aren't I* instead of *amn't I*?

19 Are the conjunctions *because, since, as* and *for* interchangeable?

20 Why do we see the past tense of some verbs spelled in two ways, such as *burned* and *burnt*?

21 Why is *go* being used these days instead of *say* in reporting speech?

22 I've just seen a film called *Marley and Me*. Shouldn't it be *Marley and I*?

23 Why do people say *whatever* on its own?

24 *What will be the result?* or *What will the result be?* Which should I use?

25 I keep coming across *Team GB*. Shouldn't it be *the GB Team*?

26 Why is *went* the past tense of *go*? (And *was* the past of *am* and *is*?)

27 Is there a difference between *I liked the story which you told* and *...that you told*?

28 Is the third person singular *-s* going to disappear?

29 Why is a possessive sometimes used before an *-ing* form, and sometimes not?

Can a be used before an uncountable noun?

> The questioner was recalling her grammar lessons, when she had been taught never to say *a knowledge, a music,* and so on. But she had just heard a native speaker say *a good knowledge of English*.

A preliminary point. Nouns aren't intrinsically countable or uncountable. Countability is *conferred* on them by the way they're used. Often-cited cases are *cake* v *a cake* and *coffee* v *a coffee,* as well as usages like *a tobacco,* meaning 'a type of tobacco'. You may think that some nouns could never vary, but it's always possible. *Chair* uncountable? A wood-eating animal might say (in a children's story), *I hate table but I love chair. Music* countable? There's a website called *Let's Make a Music.*

These may be unusual, but the point is that English allows them if the context is right, and we understand what the speaker/writer is getting at. So the question becomes: what are the contexts? The use of a preceding adjective and/or a postmodifying phrase around an uncountable noun is one, as in *a good knowledge of English,* and some grammars helpfully point this out. But some nouns are more likely to accept an adjective than others.

The most likely situation is where the noun refers to a quality or other abstraction that is attributed to a person.

> *I've had a good education.*
> *The late arrival of the train was a real annoyance.*
> *Suzie and Sasha display a charming togetherness.*
> *That's what I call a generosity of spirit.*

It's far less likely that we will see this with nouns that are impersonally abstract:

> *The business has made an important progress.*
> *There was a shoplifting at the store.*
> *The situation demonstrates an uncertainty.*

They may be less likely but they aren't impossible. Even *a progress* on its own can be found if the context motivates it, as here:

> *The progress which we saw in the 1970s is indeed a progress, and not a standing still.*

A second point: the greater the amount of premodification or postmodification, the more likely we will find the indefinite article. On its own, this sentence feels somehow incomplete:

> *She played the violin with a sensitivity.*

But don't you feel increasingly comfortable with the following?

> *She played the violin with a great sensitivity.*
> *She played the violin with a great and engaging sensitivity.*
> *She played the violin with a sensitivity that delighted the critics.*
> *She played the violin with a great and engaging sensitivity that delighted the critics.*

The more we pre/postmodify, the more we allow the particularising function of the indefinite article to operate. The modifiers make it clear that we're thinking about a specific instance of a general concept.

Do all general-concept nouns work in the same way? Some people don't accept *the teacher discovered a fresh plagiarism* and prefer something like *the teacher discovered a fresh example of plagiarism*, where the specificity is expressed by the grammar. But even an adjectiveless *a plagiarism* will be found, as in this example from *The Times* in 2005: 'The forgery – perhaps more accurately a plagiarism ...'

Postmodification is even more likely to make these nouns feel acceptable, as in these Web examples:

> *Scientific progress is a fact, but it is a progress that neutralizes itself in the process.*
> *The police reported a shoplifting of store merchandise.*
> *A project risk is an uncertainty that can be a negative or positive factor.*

A final thought: type 'a progress' into a search-engine and hundreds of thousands of instances will come up. Most are in writings which *appear* to have second-language authorship. If so, this is a further illustration of the trend to make uncountable nouns countable – a widespread feature of English as a lingua franca.

Why is the article dropped before some nouns, as in *look what baby's doing*?

> The answer brings to light some interesting features of the way English uses the definite and indefinite articles, and suggests a teaching strategy.

We always need to be prepared for unusual usages with the English article system (as seen in **15**). A proper noun doesn't usually take an article, for example, but it may do so when the aim is to single out a particular identity:

> *I'm sure I saw THE Tom Hanks at the restaurant.*
> *It wasn't a Liverpool I recognized.*

or to check on an identity, as in this snippet of dialogue:

> *I live in Baker Street.*
> *What? THE Baker Street?* (the one we know from the Sherlock Holmes stories)

There are quite a few cases where a countable noun might drop its article, often as part of the jargon of a particular subject:

> *Let's have coffee and Danish before we go.*
> *I like iPad Pro.* (in computing)
> *A is for apple, B is for bear ...* (in alphabet books)
> *The team didn't get a lot of ball in the first half.* (in sport)

In the case of *baby*, we see a noun changing its grammatical status. Normally a common noun, the omission of the article pushes it in the direction of a proper noun. One talks of *Mummy* and *Daddy*, so why not *Baby*, to complete the triad?

In this particular case, the media helped to spread the usage. *Bringing up Baby* (1938) was a popular film (*Baby* was a leopard!) as was *And Baby Makes Three* (1949). There must be hundreds of pop songs now that have an article-less *Baby* (in the extended sense of 'lover') in the title or lyrics, mostly vocative – *Bye Bye Baby, Rock Me Baby ...* . It's clearly a substitute for a proper name.

The usage isn't especially modern. Baby books and advertisements from the Victorian era show it. One ad begins *Baby will be unhappy and cross, if he ...*, and goes on to list various circumstances. The collocation *mother and baby* also has a long pedigree – as well as being the title of a popular parenting magazine.

To develop a feel for usages of this kind, a useful teaching technique is to bring the alternative forms together, such as you might read as the heading of an article.

1 *When is a baby going to sit up?*
2 *When is the baby going to sit up?*
3 *When is your baby going to sit up?*
4 *When is baby going to sit up?*
5 *When is Mary going to sit up?*

1 is impersonal, more likely to appear in a scientific article.
2 is similar, though the definite article adds a hint of familiarity
  (I know which baby I'm talking about – it's *your* baby).
3 is friendlier, with the direction now explicit – the writer is talking
  directly to the reader.
4 is communal, with the writer implying she has had the same
  experience as the reader.
5 is the most personal, as we are now talking about a real, individual
  child.

There is also what we might call a 'convenience' use, when someone doesn't know or has forgotten the name of a child, but nonetheless wants to maintain a friendly tone. This is why doctors and nurses use it a lot: *Would you put baby on the bed for me?* is more personal than *Would you put the baby on the bed for me?* which sounds more like an object – *Would you put the tray on the bed for me?* (where we would never hear *Would you put tray on the bed for me?*).

But beware! There are times when this usage can be patronizing or demeaning because it echoes baby talk. *Tell Teacher the answer* (especially if said by the teacher). *Let Nurse do it* (said by a nurse to a patient). But it can also be a source of humour. I recall a drill-sergeant in a comedy film saying sarcastically to an unhappy recruit, *Tell Sergeant all about it, then.*

Why do some teachers tell me I shouldn't begin a sentence with *and*?

> The explanation lies in the prescriptive grammar teaching of the early 19th century, but many literary examples now show how effective its use can be.

During the 19th century, schoolteachers took against the practice of beginning a sentence with *and*, presumably because they noticed the way young children often overused it. It's certainly a common feature of early story-writing style, because the children are replicating in their writing the style of everyday spoken narrative, which is full of *ands* (see **49**). This is an extract from a seven-year-old's story about what she did at the weekend:

> We went to the beach and I ate an ice-cream. And it was very windy and my hat blew away. And ...

But instead of gently weaning the children away from overuse, the teachers banned the usage altogether! Generations of children were taught they should 'never' begin a sentence with *and*, or any coordinating conjunction. Some still are.

The other main coordinating words, *but* and *or*, were also affected by the ban. Some adverbs too. In May 2015, the newly appointed Lord Chancellor in the UK government gave instructions to officials about the kind of language they ought to be using. One was a ban on beginning sentences with *however*. Of course it didn't take long for journalists to find examples of speeches where the minister himself had begun a sentence in this way. And the authors he recommended that his staff should read, such as Jane Austen, show many instances, such as this one from *Pride and Prejudice*, Chapter 17:

> It is her nature to give people the benefit of the doubt. However, Mr. Wickham's account seems to leave no doubt that Mr. Darcy is intentionally unkind.

Adverbs and conjunctions have always been used in this way, from the very beginning of the language. An initial *and* is one of the most noticeable features of Old English. We find sentences beginning with *and* in Chaucer, Shakespeare, Macaulay, and in every major writer. It's a notable feature of J R R Tolkien's style, as in the prologue to *The Lord of the Rings*, where he introduces the Hobbits:

> Hobbits had, in fact, lived quietly in Middle-earth for many long years before other folk became even aware of them. And the world being after all full of strange creatures, beyond count, these little people seemed of very little importance.

There was never any authority behind this condemnation. It isn't one of the rules laid down by the first prescriptive grammarians. Indeed, one of them, Bishop Lowth, uses dozens of examples of sentences beginning with *and*. Henry Fowler, in his *Dictionary of Modern English Usage* (1926), went so far as to call it a 'superstition'. He was right.

Of course, as with any word or grammatical feature, it's important not to overuse it. Anyone who wrote like the child above would be rightly criticised for an immature style (unless they were deliberately doing so for a literary reason). Any overused feature draws attention to itself and distracts from the meaning of what is being said. But used judiciously, an initial coordinating conjunction can add a dynamic punch to a sequence of sentences.

Take that last sentence. Note what happens if I had written it like this:

> An overused feature draws attention to itself and distracts from the meaning of what is being said, but used judiciously, an initial coordinating conjunction can add a dynamic punch to a sequence of sentences.

The meaning is the same, but the stylistic impact is very different. The words following *but* are 'buried' within the sentence as a whole. Coming second, they are read as having a subordinate relationship to the words in the first part of the sentence. Making them an independent sentence highlights them. And the reader is less likely to forget them.

Why do we say *I am*, *am I* and *I'm not*, but *aren't I* instead of *amn't I*?

> The history of the various forms of *be* brings to light a remarkable range of social and regional variables.

The history is a bit obscure, but it seems to be this. The verb forms of English have long existed in two main styles, widely recognized in English language teaching – formal or formally neutral, and informal or colloquial. Alongside *I am going* we have *I'm going*. Alongside, *are you not?* (earlier *are not you?*) we have *aren't you?* And so on.

Originally, the first person present tense of the verb *to be* followed this pattern. We find both *am I not* and *amn't I* – the latter usage still the colloquial norm today in much Irish English and some Scots. I have Irish friends and relatives who use it, and I've slipped into it myself on occasion, when visiting them. 'Amn't I a great wonder ...?' says Christy Mahon in J M Synge's *The Playboy of the Western World*, Act 2 (1907). 'Amn't I with you?' says Cissy Caffey in James Joyce's *Ulysses*, Episode 15 (1922).

But there's a pronunciation problem – the sequence of /m/ and /n/ is a little awkward, so it was a natural development to simplify the consonant cluster. The final /t/ made it more likely that the simplification would go to /ant/ rather than /amt/, because /t/ and /n/ are both articulated in the same part of the mouth – on the alveolar ridge behind the top teeth. And this is what we find in 18th-century texts, where it appears as *an't*.

The pronunciation of the /a/ vowel seems to have varied in length – sometimes short, sometimes long ('ahnt'). That would have made it sound exactly the same as the other forms in the paradigm (*aren't you/we/they*) – bearing in mind that the /r/ after the vowel wouldn't have been sounded in the newly emerging Received Pronunciation around 1800 (see **30**). So, if the first person sounded like the other persons, it would have been very natural for people to start spelling the word in the same way. It's an example of orthographic analogy. *Aren't I?* then became the standard form in British English, and *an't I?* (very popular in the 1800s) gradually fell out of use. It's widely used in US English too, but some Americans dislike it, finding it genteel.

As soon as *aren't I?* became the norm, it lost its colloquial status. So, if people could say and write *aren't I?* in formal or neutral situations, what could they say in informal situations? The stage was set for the emergence of a further alternative: *ain't*, which originally didn't have the nonstandard resonance that it has today, being widely used as a colloquialism among upper-class as well as lower-class speakers. It was probably the frequent use of this form in the literary representation of lower-class speech (especially by Charles Dickens) that eventually turned educated people against it. Henry Fowler tried to resuscitate it, in his *Dictionary of Modern English Usage* (1926), describing *ain't* as 'a natural contraction ... supplying a real want', but his view was ignored.

So, if we say *aren't I?*, why don't we now say *I aren't?* Well, a lot of people do, but only in regional dialect settings. 'I aren't frighted,' says the salesman Bob Jakin in George Eliot's *The Mill on the Floss*, Chapter 6 (1860) – a man who speaks with a strong local accent and dialect. 'I'm no reader, I aren't,' says miller Luke Mogg, in the same book (Chapter 4). It might have become part of Standard English, given that its relationship to *I am* shows the same kind of vowel lengthening that we see in *I shall* > *I shan't* and *I can* > *I can't*. But once the influential grammarians in the late 18th and early 19th centuries recognized a particular usage as the educated norm, it would have taken a sociolinguistic revolution to shift it.

Are the conjunctions *because, since,* as and *for* interchangeable?

19

> This is one of those areas of grammar where a corpus is an essential teaching aid, for the choice depends greatly on issues of context and style.

The issue arises in sentences giving a reason, such as *She was late for class because/since/as/for her watch was broken.* They can all be used, indeed, but there are frequency, stylistic, and contextual differences. *Because* (*'cos*) is by far the commonest. In samples given in *A Comprehensive Grammar of the English Language*, the percentage use of the four conjunctions was: 77 (*because*), 12 (*for*), 6 (*since*) and 5 (*as*). *For* is used in more formal style and is very rare in speech. *As* and *since* are much more common in writing, but are often avoided because of the occasional ambiguity with their temporal meaning.

> *As they were going out, they got very wet.* (*as* = *while* or *because?*)
> *Since they left, there have been many arguments.* (*since* = *after* or *because?*)

Corpus studies also show positional variation. Clauses beginning with *because, since* and *for* are much more commonly found in final position (i.e. after the main clause) – *because* clauses overwhelmingly so, especially in speech. *As* clauses tend to be more evenly balanced between initial and final position.

There's a subtle semantic difference between *because* and the other conjunctions. The sense of cause is obviously very strongly present in the form *because*; it's less emphatic in the other cases. Evidence of this comes from colloquial exchanges like this one:

> A: *Why did you buy another hat?*   B: *Because!*

This kind of usage is more recent in English; examples date only from the late 19th century. The word is being used elliptically in answer to a question and implying that a more explicit reply is being withheld for some reason. B is basically telling A: 'I don't need to give you a reason'. A related use is *just because.* A local family decided to have a get-together of as many relatives as possible. The invitation was headed: JUST BECAUSE. They felt they didn't need to explain further.

Even more recent is a prepositional use of *because* without *of*, as in this Twitter message: *Going to bed early because exhausted*. Some of these constructions could be analysed as a shortened form of a clause (*because I am exhausted*), but in most cases it isn't possible to predict exactly what has been left out, as in this tweet: *Not home yet because trains*. Either way, its succinct, lively tone has given it a wide appeal, and its fashionable status online led to it being voted a Word of the Year in 2013 (American Dialect Society). It's even become a book title: Gretchen McCulloch called her book on digital language *Because Internet* (2019).

You may also hear *Because why?* or *'Cos why?* used in modern English, as a colloquial substitution for the simple *Why?* especially when someone is arguing back. This seems to have regional origins. A Kentish dialect dictionary from 1887 quotes an argument between some youngsters:

A: *No it ain't.*   B: *'Cos why?*   A: *'Cos it ain't.*

The instances cited in Joseph Wright's *English Dialect Dictionary* (1906) – the first large-scale dialect survey of the British Isles – are geographically some distance from each other: from Derbyshire to Kent to Somerset, and also in Ireland. The construction must be an old one, to have spread so widely, and indeed Wright quotes one example from the 14th century.

Note also that, if you want to introduce stylistic variation into your speech or writing, English provides several other alternatives for expressing reason, such as:

With bad weather coming, I've decided to close the store. (= Because bad weather is coming ...)
What with the bad weather coming ...
Seeing (that) the bad weather is coming ...

And there are more complex (and often more formal) constructions such as:

Inasmuch as the bad weather is coming ...

You can replace *inasmuch* by *insofar* (or *in so far*), *in view of*, *on account of*, *owing to*, *due to* ... . Plenty of choice, then, for the aspiring stylist.

Quirk, R., Greenbaum, S., Leech, G. and J. Svartvik. (1985) *A Comprehensive Grammar of the English Language*. London: Pearson.

Why is the past tense of some verbs spelled in two ways, such as *burned* and *burnt*?

20

> Is this variation just a matter of stylistic choice and regional preference? It turns out that grammatical aspect is implicated too.

Monosyllabic past-time forms such as *burned*, *learned* and *smelled* are usually spelled with *-ed* in American English, whereas in British English we find *burnt*, *learnt* and *smelt* as well. There's a subtle aspectual difference of meaning. The *-ed* form is more likely to be used when the duration of an action or the process of acting is being emphasized, and the *-t* form when something happens once, or takes up very little time, or the focus is on the result of a process rather than on the process itself. So we're more likely to find *The fire burned for three days*, not *The fire burnt for three days*. A sudden event is likely to be spelled with *-t*: *I burnt the toast*. And certainly it's going to be *I burnt my finger on the oven*.

The best way of testing this distinction is to compare pairs of examples. In *The house burnt down*, the implication is that the event took place quite quickly, whereas *burned* is more likely in *The house burned for days*. The adjective, though, never allows variation: it's always *burnt toast*, never *burned toast*.

Similarly, *I've dreamed all my life of living in Scotland* is more likely than *I dreamt all my life of living in Scotland*. *Dreamt* tends to be used for single, short, and determinate instances of dreaming, where the dreamer is asleep (*I dreamt last night I was in Italy*); *dreamed* tends to be used for a more continuous and indefinable dreaming, where the dreamer is awake (*I dreamed of meeting you all week*). There is some overlap, though not in contexts where the 'awake' sense is clear, such as daydreaming, which gives rise to *I daydreamed for hours*, not *I daydreamt for hours*. It isn't a hard-and-fast rule, but it does help to explain the relative frequency of different items. *Spilt* is much more likely than *spilled* because the action of spilling is usually short. *Learned* is much more likely than *learnt* because the action of learning usually takes some time.

Not all verbs have retained the two spellings in Standard English. For instance, there are no instances of *boilt* in the *Oxford English Dictionary*, though there was a great deal of spelling variation in the early centuries of its use. But regional dictionaries do show examples, especially in Scotland, Ulster, northern England, the Isle of Man, and parts of the USA (especially those influenced by Scots-Irish settlers). A Scots poetic example from 1790: *Twa pints o' weel-boilt solid sowins* ('Two pints of well-boiled oat-meal beverage'). And Joseph Wright in the *English Dialect Dictionary* has several examples from northern England, such as *He brought eaut a fresh-boilt pestil* (*eaut* 'out'; *pestil* 'a pig's fore-leg').

Usage changes, though. If we explore the way the two forms have developed over time, using Google Ngrams (based on their occurrence in books since 1800) we find that *spoiled, learned, leaned* and *leaped* have always been well ahead of *spoilt, learnt, leant* and *leapt*, whereas *knelt* far outnumbers *kneeled*, presumably because the action of kneeling down is short. But something interesting happened around the end of the 19th century. Before that, *burnt, spilt* and *spelt* were the more frequent forms, but not afterwards. *Smelt* stayed more frequent until the 1940s, and then *smelled* shot ahead. Of course, these are very crude statistics which don't take account of regional differences, aspectual subtleties, or differences between parts of speech. But they do show that this is a highly dynamic area of English usage.

Why is *go* being used these days instead of *say* in reporting speech?

21

It's not just 'these days'. This use of *go* has been around for quite a while, though it has certainly increased in frequency in recent decades.

The earliest recorded instances are over 150 years old. The *Oxford English Dictionary* defines it thus: 'to utter (the noise indicated) with direct speech', and cites Charles Dickens in 1837:

'Yo-yo-yo-yo-yoe,' went the first boy. 'Yo-yo-yo-yoe!' went the second.

Past tense and present tense uses are found throughout the 20th century, with the present tense usage increasing.

This use of *go* is technically called a *quotative* – a form that acts as an introduction to direct speech, functioning in a similar way to the use of quotation marks. Not having punctuation marks available when we speak, we've devised various ways of alerting listeners to the fact that we're about to say something which would need quotation marks in writing, such as making a gesture in the air with the first two fingers of each hand, or – more conveniently – using an introductory word such as *like*, *says* or *goes*.

Say is the traditional form, of course. So why has an alternative usage developed? An analysis of actual usage provides the clue. Here are some examples:

Two minutes in, he goes, 'Wow, this is strenuous' and stopped.
And he goes, 'Gosh, I've never seen you in one of those'...
And I go, 'Hello, this is odd'...
And Terry goes, '(whistles)'...

Note how the direct speech begins with an interjection or similar vocal effect. In one study (see the reference below), it was found that 76 percent of uses of quotative *go* occurred with a following vocal effect, often with accompanying gestures or facial expressions. The function is sometimes described as 'mimetic' – the speaker is trying to recreate exactly the audio-visual character of the discourse being reported.

A longer extract from the corpus used in that study shows something different (I omit the addressee's reactions). The speaker is telling a story about how he was mistaken for a woman because of his long hair:

> the other day I went into a bar and this guy asked me to dance, and all he saw was my hair, and he goes 'do you wanna dance' ? I turn around and go 'what' ? and he goes 'do you wanna dance' ? I go 'no no'. he goes 'oh oh I'm sorry'. I go 'yeah you better be'…

Here we see some other features that motivate a *go* usage. It's a dramatic narrative, which the speaker is trying to make as vivid as possible. The speaker is critically involved in what went on. The interaction involves a high level of emotion. And this explains why the usage has developed: it offers a dramatic alternative to *say*. *Say* is used when the language is more factual; *go* when the speaker in the narrative is more involved in the action.

(1) *So Anna says, 'It's time we were leaving.'*
(2) *So Anna goes, 'It's time we were leaving.'*

In (1), the speaker is reporting what happened. In (2), there's a greater dynamic force: something has just happened to make Anna say this.

I see the quotative use of *go* as the emergence of a fresh expressive option in informal speech. And we see a similar development when the verb *to be* or the particle *like* is used in the same way, as in

So I was, 'Really?'
So I was, like, 'Really?'

All these usages become noticeable because, when people are telling a conversation they find dramatic, they tend to use them repeatedly – just as they would with *say* in less dramatic circumstances. They can attract criticism as a result, and poor *like* is often condemned when someone seems unable to tell a story without using it after every few words. As with any habit, overuse draws attention to itself and distracts from the message.

Buchstaller, I. (2013) *Quotatives: New Trends and Sociolinguistic Implications*. John Wiley and Sons, Inc.

I've just seen a film called *Marley and Me*. Shouldn't it be *Marley and I*?

22

This innocent question raises one of the most contentious topics in the history of English grammar, and the answer takes us well beyond the world of cinema.

Both patterns are used in film and book titles. Along with *Marley and Me* we find *Monkey and Me*, *My Bump and Me*, and more. The alliteration of *m/b* and *m* is noticeable. On the other hand, we find the cult film *Withnail and I*, the classic *The King and I*, and others. There's even a minimal pair. In 2009, an exhibition of Murray Close's photographs from the set of Withnail was called *Withnail and Me*.

Plainly there's a choice, which will depend on the general feelings you have about the use of *me* and *I* in everyday use. Most people sense a formality difference, with *I* more formal than *me*. There's also a pragmatic issue arising out of the way *I* has been privileged in prescriptive teaching over the past 200 years, so that some people are scared of using *me* – notwithstanding the fact that the *and me* or *me and* constructions have a history of usage dating from the 14th century.

Note also that the pressures operating on pronouns when used in a coordinate construction differ from when they are used in isolation – which is why people who would never normally use *I* after a preposition (as in *give it to I*) or as an object (*you helped I*) do so unconsciously in coordination (as in *between you and I*).

If it had been left to itself, *me* would have been the normal usage in the short texts that constitute titles, as it is in other self-contained pieces of 'block language', where *me* is the norm, especially if the sentences are exclamatory in character. None of the following allow *I*:

Dear me! Goodness me!　　*Silly me! Funny me!*
Me go by train? Never!　　*Me and my big mouth!*

Me? (= do you mean me?)   *Me too.*
I got told off – and me only trying to be helpful.
Me in Blackpool. (as in a photograph caption)

But of course it wasn't left to itself. From the 18th century on, prescriptive grammarians insisted that *I* was correct in sentences like *It is I,* and *me* was incorrect, introducing a Latin rule which went against the natural idiom of English. This produced generations of conflicting intuitions and a sensitivity to their use which is still with us. The uncertainty that people feel is a direct result of the attempt to implement that artificial rule. They don't like to use *I* in everyday speech because it's felt to be too formal. On the other hand, they find *me* uncomfortable because they've been told that it's wrong.

It's not surprising, then, to see the rise of alternatives – especially *myself*. Usages such as *Jane and myself went to the cinema* and *send the parcel to myself* are on the increase – an ancient usage, which remained alive only in a few regional varieties, notably Irish English, but which is increasingly encountered now, though with some regional variation. It's already beginning to appear in book and film titles, as in *Oscar Wilde and Myself* and *My Father and Myself.*

What has been unexpected is to hear other reflexive pronouns following the same pattern, as in *I'll write to yourself soon* and *I saw herself in town.* I've also begun to see them in formal writing, as in this recent communication from a tax office: *There may be occasions where HMRC has to issue notification to yourself and your agent.*

But not everyone finds these usages elegant or acceptable, so it would be wise for the time being to respect the traditional pronoun use in teaching situations.

Why does *I* have a capital letter?

When *I* developed as a single sound out of Old English *ic/ich,* there was uncertainty about how to write it. Various manuscript versions were proposed, such as *i, I, j, y,* and *Y.* Printers standardized on *I,* probably to avoid a confusion with *i,* which was also used in numerals, as in *iii* (=3).

Why do people say *whatever* on its own?

23

And what part of speech is it?

As with many words, the part of speech (or word class) depends on how it's used. Take *round*, which can be an adjective (*the round table*), a noun (*it's your round*), a verb (*we rounded the bend*), an adverb (*we went round*), and a preposition (*round the corner*). *Whatever* is just as various.

- In sentences like *Whatever happened?* it's a pronoun. Pronouns take the place of noun phrases, as in *It happened – An explosion happened*. This is also the usage when part of a sentence is omitted, as in *Whatever next!* (= 'Whatever will happen next?').

- When it's used to introduce a clause, we get sentences like *I love whatever she writes* or *Whatever he says will upset me*. Here it's a subordinating conjunction.

- When it's used along with a noun, we can't call it a pronoun any more. Now it says something about the noun. *Wear **whatever dress** you like*. Words used like this (*whichever* and *what* are two more) were called 'adjectives' in old grammars, but that isn't a good label because they don't act like adjectives in other ways. Today we would call them 'determiners' (like *the* and *my*), because they 'determine' the character of the noun – making it interrogative, in this case. It's an 'interrogative determiner', here.

- It's used as an 'emphatic determiner' after a noun when there's a negative word before it, as in *They had no reason whatever to leave*. *Whatsoever* and *at all* (see **10**) do the same job.

In informal speech, since the 1960s, a usage has grown up in which the relative clause has been shortened, so that only the pronoun is left. *We'll go by bus or train or whatever* (= 'or whatever else might be available') evolved into *We'll go by bus or train – whatever!* Related words were being used in the same way. *We'll go to Paris or Vienna or wherever*.

Eventually, the *wh-* words came to be used on their own. *Whatever! Wherever! Whenever!* The speaker doesn't want to say anything more about the subject. They're often used as a one-word response, meaning 'if you say so' or 'have it your own way', conveying an attitude of impatience or indifference.

Now when a word loses its original grammatical identity, and starts being used in an independent way, it no longer makes much sense to talk about it as a part of speech. Lots of words are like this. What part of speech is *Thanks* or *Hi!* or *Hello*? They are really acting like mini-sentences, but without the sort of grammatical structure we usually find in a sentence. Modern grammars sometimes call them 'minor sentences'. Dictionaries have to give them some label, so they do – but it's a bit of a cheat, really, to talk about such words as parts of speech at all.

Whatever is one of the most recent words to achieve independent status in this way. When it's on its own, it tends to be used as an exclamatory sentence, the intonation (with a high unstressed *what* and a lower level tone on *ever*) conveying a dismissive force. Because it often expresses an attitude, similar in effect to such words as *phooey!* it's actually very close to what grammars call an 'interjection'. Since the 1990s, colloquial short forms have developed, especially in online responses: *whatev whenev, wherev*, and using a diminutive *-s* suffix – *whatevs, whenevs, wherevs*.

All of this applies to speech. In writing there's an additional complication. When *whatever* is used as an intensifier (along with *whoever, however, wherever,* and all the *-soever* words – *whatsoever, wheresoever,* etc.), there's been a trend to separate the *ever* from the first part: *What ever did he mean?* It was Henry Fowler who first thought this was a good idea, in his *Dictionary of Modern English Usage* (1926), suggesting that it drew attention to the emphasis, and several people followed his lead. But modern dictionaries usually recommend that the word be set solid.

What will be the result? or What will the result be? Which should I use?

24

> This question makes us consider important stylistic factors, especially the role of a construction's length in deciding on its acceptability.

Whenever there's an alternative situation like this, you can be fairly certain that stylistic issues are involved. Both word orders are possible. The question is to determine the circumstances in which each is more likely to be used.

There's no doubt that in written English the *Wh- will be* construction is preferred. Even allowing for all the uncertainties that come when searching for a string in a search engine (such as duplication of data on different sites), the following results are striking (for a Google search in 2020):

> *What will be the result?* 34 million hits
> *What will the result be?* 266 thousand hits

And a similar huge difference is found with *Who will be the captain?* v *Who will the captain be?*, *Where will be the next solar eclipse?* v *Where will the next solar eclipse be?*, and so on.

On the other hand, in speech we frequently hear such sentences with an end-placed *be*: *Who will the next James Bond be?* And there's even a folk rhyme, spoken and sung, with a repeated refrain reinforcing this usage:

> O dear, what can the matter be? O dear, what can the matter be?
> O dear, what can the matter be? Johnny's so long at the fair.

Compare these with some typical sentences from the Web where the verb phrase is kept unified:

> *Who will be the next person to walk on the moon?*
> *What will be the result of having your vehicle properly serviced by a reputable garage?*

The difference in length is striking. People evidently want to add extra information after the noun, and the longer this 'extra' goes on, the less likely we will see the verb postponed to the end. Compare:

What will the effect of Covid-19 be?
What will the long-term effect of Covid-19 be?
What will the long-term effect of Covid-19 on international markets be?
What will the long-term effect of Covid-19 on home businesses, international markets and the general economy be?

There comes a point where the distance between *will* and *be* is so great that the sentence starts to be difficult to process. At that point, there's pressure to keep the verb phrase united. And from an intonational point of view, as the sentence becomes longer it becomes rhythmically awkward to integrate the final *be*. Try saying that last example aloud, and you'll feel the problem. Do you make *be* a separate tone unit? Do you introduce a slight pause before it?

When a usage is affected by gradually increasing length, there's no absolute rule. People will have different intuitions about when it sounds or reads better to move from one usage to the other. On the whole, the shorter sentences will be heard in informal conversation, so we're more likely to encounter end-placed *be* there. In printed English, the sentences will be longer, and tend to be more literary and formal, so a unified verb phrase will be more likely there, especially if the verb phrase becomes more complex, as in: *What will have been the effect?*, *What could have been the matter?*

Perhaps that is why some teachers feel the need to correct, as happened in the case of the person who first asked me this question. An end-placed *be* might feel too colloquial for a written context. A unified verb might feel too contrived for a spoken context. However, it's perfectly possible to make *will be* sentences more informal, by using a contracted auxiliary, as in: *What'll be the effect ...? Who'll be the next person ...?* And it's possible to make an end-placed *be* sound more formally rhetorical, by speaking the sentence more slowly and placing extra weight on *be* by giving it a strong stress. With stylistic questions, there are always other options.

I keep coming across *Team GB.*
Shouldn't it be *the GB Team?*

> This is the brand name of the British Olympic Association, and it caught the public attention.

The usage 'Team X' had been used sporadically in the 1990s, but it was the Olympic usage that became widely used a decade later. Soon people were talking about *Team USA*, *Team Canada* and others.

It then began to develop other applications. *Team* in sport normally means the players. We then see it used for the people who support a player: a Web headline read *Team Murray: The men and women behind Britain's No 1* (referring to the tennis star Andy Murray). It then left sport behind, so that we saw *Team Obama*, *Team Trump*, and the like, with some of the labels having an identity in social media.

The next step saw a development of the competitive notion underlying teams: which side are you supporting? That led to juxtapositions such as these, taken from the Web in 2019:

> *Are you Team Johnson or Team Hunt?* (to be the next Tory Party leader)
> *Are you Team Batman or Team Superman?*
> *Are you Team Beatles or Team Stones?*

The meaning is now very general: 'a member of a group which supports someone'. And the last stage was when it ceased to be animate. In a 2019 website about the merits of competing beverages, we read: *Are you team coffee, or team tea?*

The grammar is unusual, but not unique. The construction has a superficial resemblance to the way English sometimes puts adjectives after the noun – a usage that goes back to Middle English, where we see such borrowings from French as *battle royal* and *court martial*. Today we see the pattern in a host of culinary terms, such as *Eggs Benedict*, *Peach Melba* and *Chicken Kiev*, as well as the names of firms, such as *Club Med* and *Sports Direct*.

But *Team* is not an adjective; it's a noun. The construction would thus seem to have more in common with what in grammar would usually be described as 'restrictive apposition': NOUN more specifically identified as NOUN. So: 'the team which is identified as GB'. This has been in English for a long time:

Mount Everest (= the mountain known as Everest)
Queen Elizabeth (= the Queen who in this case is Elizabeth)
the number six (= the number that is six)
the year 2009 (= the year that is 2009)
Platform 3 (= the platform that is labelled 3)

But there is a difference. *Team GB* is reversible as *the GB team*. This doesn't work with the above. We do not say *the 3 platform*, *the Elizabeth Queen*. The reversed word order gives the usage a rhetorical punch. And the omission of the article is a factor too. Compare the different effect of:

We support Team GB.
We support the GB Team.

The zero article makes it like many other identifying expressions, such as *Operation Desert Storm*, *Generation X*, *Health Canada* and *Mission Impossible* (a spoken form of *Mission: Impossible*), all of which allow the alternative word order. There is no difference in meaning between *Team GB* and the *GB Team*, but there is a clear difference in stylistic effect.

Having said that, note that there can sometimes be a semantic difference between a preposed and a postposed noun. *Team A* is the first of several teams to be mentioned (there is also *Team B*, *Team C*, etc). *The A Team* (or *A-team*) has to be 'the best team' – as in the name of the 1980s television series.

Team GB has attracted controversy, indeed, but for political rather than linguistic reasons. The organization defines itself as the 'Great Britain and Northern Ireland Olympic team' – so strictly speaking it should be *Team UK*.

Why is *went* the past tense of *go*? (And *was* the past of *am* and *is*?)

26

I think the story of *went* is one of the most fascinating in the history of English, because what happened was so unusual.

Normally, verbs form their past tense in a regular way, as we know from *walk – walked, jump – jumped*, and thousands more. And, as every learner painfully knows, English has a few hundred verbs that form their past tense in an irregular way: *take – took, come – came*, and so on. The vowel changes have a history that goes right back to the Germanic languages, but at least the relationship between the two forms is recognisable through the consonants, which stay the same: *t–k, c–m*. But there is no such continuity between *go* and *went*. What happened?

The story begins in the 14th century. Before that, the verb *go* in Old English – *gan* – had a past tense that was irregular: *eode*. Why this form went out of fashion is anybody's guess, but the fact is that during the 1300s people stopped using it, apart from in some regional dialects, and *went* took its place. Where did *went* come from? There was another verb with a closely related meaning: *wend*. To *wend* meant to go with unhurried movement, in an indirect or meandering course. It still exists today, as in: *We watched the procession wend slowly out of sight*, or in the collocation with *way*: *they began to wend their way home*. The past tense of *wend* was *went*, and this is the form that entered the paradigm of *go*, becoming a companion to *goes, goeth* (see **28**), *going* and *gone*.

We then see the curious situation of two verbs having the same past tense form. *Went* was used for both *wend* and *go*. Despite the possibility of confusion, people evidently lived with it for quite some time. The situation wasn't resolved until the end of the 16th century, when a new, regular past tense of *wend* emerged – *wended*. We now say: *They wended their way home*.

Linguistics has given us a technical term for cases like this, where one form is replaced by another derived from a different stem: *suppletion* –

the word relates to *supplement* and *supply*. The process can be seen in dozens of languages. It doesn't happen very often in English, but *went* isn't unique. We see it in the relation between *good, better* and *best* (not *gooder* and *goodest*), *bad, worse* and *worst* (not *badder* and *baddest*), *one* and *first* (not *oneth*), *two* and *second* (not *twoth*), and above all in the various forms of the verb *to be*, the most irregular verb in English.

The irregularity arises because, very early in the history of the Indo-European languages, three different verbs with related meanings came together. A verb which scholars think had a very general meaning of 'exist' gave rise to *am, are* and *is*. Another had the meaning of 'become' or 'grow', and this gave rise to *be, being* and *been*. And a third verb, with the meaning 'remain' or 'stay', resulted in *was* and *were*. Many other languages display similarly irregular paradigms. Why people opted for the particular combination of forms we know today is a mystery.

Standard English has retained the irregularities; but in many regional dialects we see simplifications. In the UK West Midlands, for example, we can hear *am* used for all present tense forms: *I am, you am*, etc. In the UK south-west, *be* became the norm: *I be, you be*, etc. And in Ireland, Newfoundland, the Caribbean, several parts of the USA, and especially in African American Vernacular English, we can hear *be* used for all present tense persons, but expressing a habitual meaning. *The car be in the garage* means 'The car is usually in the garage'. *I be tired* means 'I'm often tired'.

Is there a difference between *I liked the story which you told* and *...that you told*?

27

Both are possible sentences in Standard English – and of course there's a third option: to omit the pronoun: *I liked the story you told*. So what are the factors which/that motivate the choice?

The fact that there's a choice at all upset prescriptive grammarians in the 18th century, and they spent a lot of futile energy trying to get rid of it. There has been variation in the use of relative pronouns since late Middle English. As Henry Fowler remarks in his *Dictionary of Modern English Usage* (1926):

> The relations between *that*, *who*, & *which*, have come to us from our forefathers as an odd jumble, & plainly show that the language has not been neatly constructed by a master-builder who could create each part to do the exact work required of it, neither overlapped nor overlapping; far from that, its parts have had to grow as they could.

(As you see, he had an idiosyncratic way of writing *and*.) He spends six pages trying to sort things out before deciding that it wasn't going to be possible.

The changes are still going on. In recent years, *that* has come to be used much more than *which*, and the use of *which* is noticeably diminishing. In one corpus-based study of American academic texts, the use of *which* dropped from around 70 percent in a corpus compiled in 1961 to around 20 percent in a corpus compiled in 1992. The zero form, which is very frequent in informal speech, shows much less change.

Why is this happening? Several stylistic factors are involved.

Which has long been associated with more formal styles of expression, and *that* with informality, so it's been affected by what's been called the increasing 'colloquialization' of written English in recent decades.

Constructions that a generation ago would have been thought inappropriate in a print setting (such as the contracted forms of verbs) are now seen much more often – as in this paragraph.

In writing, *which* is weightier, taking up more visual space than *that*. *That* is sometimes described as being a 'lighter' word to use and preferred as sentences become more complex in structure. Auditorily, *that* can be said faster, as the *a* can be replaced by schwa (the vowel sound heard in *the*), whereas no such reduction takes place with *which*. Similarly, *that* can be followed by a contracted form, whereas *which* can't:

> *Did you see the car that's parked in the street?*
> *Did you see the car which is parked in the street?*

However, often the decision about which word to use depends on the circumstances of an individual sentence. A particularly important stylistic factor is the avoidance of repetition. If one of the words is already being used, people tend not to repeat it. I would never write *That is the answer that I prefer,* but *That is the answer which I prefer.* Similarly, I would avoid *Which is the answer which you prefer?* and instead write *Which is the answer that you prefer?* Speech is less predictable in this respect.

The corpus studies show a great deal of variation relating to genre. The informality of *that* is shown by its greater frequency in conversation and in fiction, whereas *which* is more often used in nonfiction and formal speech, such as news reporting.

It's difficult to generalize, therefore. But, on the whole, *that* seems to be taking over the function of *which* in restrictive relative clauses. But note: *restrictive*. In *non-restrictive* relative clauses (shown by the commas in writing and by a separate intonation contour in speech), *that* is not possible.

I want to sell my car, which has a red stripe down the side.
(= I have only one car.)
I want to sell my car which/that has a red stripe down the side.
(= I have more than one car, and I'm not selling the other one.)

Is the third person singular -s going to disappear?

28

Where did it come from? Who's actually dropping it?
This form has a fascinating history.

All over the English-speaking dialect world, we hear people dropping the -s ending in the third person indicative present tense (3s). It's normal to hear it in pidgin and creole Englishes, and it's a well-known feature of African American Vernacular English (AAVE). Rap and hip-hop music have made it familiar to millions, and for many young people it's 'cool' to drop the -s in everyday colloquial speech, even though it was never historically a part of their dialect. Two-year-old children leave it out when they're starting to talk. And of course it's the usual practice for all second language learners, until they realize that this is one of those annoying rules that has to be followed to produce acceptable Standard English.

It's a relic of the inflectional system of Old English, where the 3s form ended in a consonant written as -ð and pronounced like the voiceless *th* in modern *thin*. We see it still in religious writing (*goeth*, *hath*) and often hear it on stage in plays by Shakespeare and his contemporaries. But around the 10th century we see a new ending appear in texts written in the North of England, -s. This became widespread during the early Middle Ages, and by the 15th century the usage had reached the Midlands and South, the areas that had greatest influence on the development of Standard English.

Where did it come from? There's no sign of it elsewhere in Old English, so it must have come from outside; and as the only influence in the North of England was from Scandinavia, it must have been the result of contact between Anglo-Saxons and Danish incomers. The strange thing is that the equivalent form in Old Norse didn't have an -s ending: 'he/she tells' was *hann/hon telr*. Scholars therefore think that the -s arose as a result of a learning error typical when languages come into contact. In one theory, Anglo-Saxons heard -s used in other forms of the Old Norse verb and thought it belonged to the 3s construction as well. Or maybe Danes mispronounced the *th* as *s* – as still happens today, when learners find the articulation difficult – and the Anglo-Saxons eventually copied it.

Either way, 3s became the educated norm, and from the 16th century any other way of expressing that person in the present tense was found only in dialects. With one exception – in the subjunctive, where we hear *God save the Queen, Suffice it to say,* and other set phrases, as well as in some types of subordinate clause in formal style (*I insist that he go now ...*). But the -*s* ending didn't disappear entirely from regional speech. It's been observed sometimes even in AAVE, in sentences such as *That's the way it be's*. And some dialects have generalised it to other persons, as in *I be's,* etc. in parts of Ireland.

It's never possible to predict long-term usage, when it comes to language, but I can't see 3s disappearing from Standard English in the foreseeable future. Both forms will stylistically co-exist, with learners needing to become aware of the different contexts of use – as they do when distinguishing formal, informal, scientific, religious and other styles.

Is 3s ever *useful* in Standard English? Yes, with invariable nouns like *sheep*. Compare:

Your sheep looks lovely. (a pet sheep, perhaps)
Your sheep look lovely. (presumably a whole field full)

There aren't many nouns like this: a few animals, such as *deer, cod, moose, salmon, trout,* and a few collectives, such as *offspring, species, aircraft, spacecraft.* So 3s isn't totally redundant in Standard English. If it does ever disappear, an alternative will have to emerge to handle these cases – maybe new plurals (*sheeps, aircrafts ...*). And the rappers would soon find another way of being linguistic rebels.

Why is a possessive sometimes used before an *-ing* form, and sometimes not?

29

This raises one of the most important topics in English grammar: the contrast between formal and informal usage.

The questioner is thinking of contrasts like these:

Poss: *I was impressed by his/my uncle's/Ivan's travelling by train.*
NoPoss: *I was impressed by him/my uncle/Ivan travelling by train.*

NoPoss is the older construction, recorded since the Middle Ages, and widely used. But 18th-century prescriptive grammarians felt that the possessive was more elegant and grammatically correct, and this view was given the strongest possible support in the 20th century by the influential Henry Fowler in his *Dictionary of Modern English Usage* (1926). In one of his strongest statements, he describes the earlier usage as 'grammatically indefensible', and asserts that 'every just man who will abstain from (it) ... retards the process of corruption'.

The effect of the prescriptive attitude was to associate *Poss* with a formal style, especially in writing. This is especially felt when the *-ing* construction is used as the subject of a clause, as in *travelling by train is inconvenient*, where we have the choice of:

Ivan's travelling by train is inconvenient.
Ivan travelling by train is inconvenient.

And the formal/informal contrast is really noticeable when there's an initial pronoun:

My travelling by train is inconvenient.
Me travelling by train is inconvenient.

But note that the informal tone of the NoPoss construction is somewhat diminished if it is 'buried' later in the sentence:

It is inconvenient, my travelling by train.
It is inconvenient, me travelling by train.

The contrast is not just a stylistic one. The two constructions convey different emphases, which emerge more clearly when the sentences are seen in context. Poss makes us focus on the noun phrase or pronoun, whereas NoPoss transfers our focus to the verb phrase. So we're more likely to see Poss used in a context where there's an implied contrast with some other noun phrase, such as:

> *I was impressed by my uncle's travelling by train and my aunt's agreeing to it.*

NoPoss is more likely to be used in a context where the implied contrast is with some other verb phrase, such as:

> *I was impressed by my uncle travelling by train and enjoying it.*

These trends are reinforced if other elements are added to the sentence. If we insert an adjective, then this pushes the *-ing* form clearly in the direction of a noun, and the construction now looks like a familiar possessive noun phrase:

> *Ivan's daily travelling by train is inconvenient.*
> *Ivan's daily travel by train is inconvenient.*

Conversely, adding an adverbial pushes the *-ing* form in the direction of a verb:

> *Ivan routinely travelling by train is inconvenient.*
> *Ivan is routinely travelling by train.*

In each case the alternative construction is less likely.

Pronunciation is another factor that influences which construction will be used. The *s* used in Poss can make a sentence slightly more difficult to articulate. *Him showing me* is easier to say than *his showing me*, where formal speakers would want to avoid any hint of assimilation of the *s* towards the *sh*. And if the speaker wants to add emphasis, then *IVAN travelling by train is inconvenient* is more likely than *IVAN's travelling by train is inconvenient*. Factors like these increase the frequency of the NonPoss construction in everyday speech, and that reinforces the motivation to make Poss the construction of choice in formal writing.

This is a tricky area of grammar, and it raises several general issues. We're talking about trends here, not absolute rules. And it draws attention to the importance of seeing sentences in context. All too often people try to rate the acceptability of a sentence in isolation. This may be convenient in a textbook, but it's always worthwhile trying to find examples of the competing constructions in a corpus, especially when testing hypotheses about formality.

C: Pronunciation

Questions about pronunciation range from very general ones about variation and change, especially in regional accents, to very specific ones about individual sounds, words and intonations. For this section, I've selected questions that reflect this range, and illustrated the kind of regional and social issues that any study of pronunciation raises.

30 Where did RP (Received Pronunciation) come from?

31 Have English accents changed in Britain in recent years?

32 What is this 'Estuary English' that I read about?

33 Why do some people say *after<u>noon</u>* and some say *<u>after</u>noon*?

34 Why do people drop the final g when they say *good morning*?

35 Why am I hearing so many high rising tones on statements these days?

30 Where did RP (Received Pronunciation) come from?

And what does 'received' mean exactly?

For the first thousand years of English in Britain, there was no such thing as a 'standard' accent. People spoke in different ways, reflecting their regional backgrounds, regardless of their level of education or social class. In Shakespeare's day, having a broad regional accent didn't stop you becoming powerful in the kingdom, as illustrated by Francis Drake and Walter Raleigh, both said to have had strong Devonshire accents. Indeed, you could become king with a regional accent, as happened in 1603 when James VI of Scotland became James I of England, and Scottish accents echoed through the corridors of power.

RP didn't exist in 16th-century England. People in the south-east – the home of the Court, the Church, and Oxford and Cambridge universities – of course considered their regional accent(s) to be superior to those spoken elsewhere. And by the 18th century, the accent used in these places, as it later evolved, gradually became the pronunciation to imitate if one wanted to appear cultured. By the end of the century, the notion of a 'posh' accent had emerged as a result of the elocution movement, which grew to satisfy the demands of an up-and-coming middle class wanting to speak in a way that wouldn't be criticised by 'polite' society. The first dictionary of English pronunciation, compiled by John Walker in 1791, introduces the term by which it later came to be known:

> For though the pronunciation of London is certainly erroneous in many words, yet, upon being compared with that of any other place, it is undoubtedly the best; that is, not only the best by courtesy, and because it happens to be the pronunciation of the capital, but best by a better title; that of being more generally received.

'Received' meant the kind of pronunciation that had come to be socially accepted because it had been passed down by the 'higher orders' in society from one generation to the next. And it was this sense that later appealed to the phonetician Alexander Ellis, who in 1869 described the

English cultured accent as *Received Pronunciation*. The term became really well known when it was taken up some decades later by the University of London professor of phonetics Daniel Jones, and widely abbreviated to *RP*.

Walker made it very clear in the Preface to his dictionary that this cultured accent needed to be clearly distinct from other regional accents, and his recommendations showed speakers how they could maintain the divide, by stressing words in the 'right' way, and giving vowels and consonants the 'right' value. If Cockney speakers dropped their *h*'s, in words like *happy*, then speakers of RP should not. If people in the provinces pronounced their *r* after a vowel, in words like *heart*, then speakers of RP should not. The actual character of RP developed as a partly conscious and partly unconscious attempt to differentiate cultured speakers from those of the 'lower orders'. And it became the voice of English worldwide after it became the preferred pronunciation in the public schools, and after the products of those schools – the missionaries, diplomats, civil servants and military officers – took the language around the world during the formation of the British Empire.

In 1922, when the BBC began, its founder Lord Reith recognized the status of RP as a unifying force. Although himself a Scot, he realized that broadcasting needed to use an accent that would be the most widely understood, and the only one that could achieve that aim, he felt, was the one that had become the educated norm. It would certainly be the accent that would be expected among those people who could afford to buy one of the new wireless sets. And it stayed that way until social pressure during the second half of the 20th century introduced a wider range of accents in broadcasting (see **31**).

Have English accents changed in Britain in recent years?

> Accents never stand still. But change involves more than replacing one sound by another; it also alters the way we value them.

There have been two major changes. The attitude of people towards accents has altered in ways that were unpredictable a generation or two ago; and some accents have changed their phonetic character very noticeably over the same period.

The main change in attitude has affected Received Pronunciation (RP), which during the 20th century became the uncontested prestige accent of Britain. For many it was the public auditory image of the country, still valued today for its associations with the Second World War years, the royal family, and leading classical actors such as Laurence Olivier. In 1980, when the BBC made its first attempt to use a regionally accented announcer on Radio 4, the decision aroused such listener opposition that it was quickly reversed.

Twenty-five years later, things had changed. In August 2005, the BBC devoted a whole week to a celebration of the accents and dialects of the British Isles: the *Voices* project. This was an attempt to take an auditory snapshot of the way Britain was sounding at the beginning of the new millennium. Every BBC regional radio station was invited to take part, and local presenters arranged recordings of the diversity within their area, as well as programmes which explored the history and nature of local accents and dialects. It was institutional recognition of a fundamental change in attitudes to regional speech that had taken place in Britain. There's now a much greater readiness to value and celebrate linguistic diversity than there was a generation ago.

As far as broadcasting was concerned, it was the rapid growth of local commercial radio that fostered the new linguistic climate. Regional radio gained audience (and national radio lost it) by meeting the interests of local populations, and these new audiences liked their presenters to speak as they did. At the same time, national listening and viewing figures remained strong for such series as 'The Archers' and 'Coronation Street', where local accents were privileged.

Soon, non-RP accents began to be used as part of the 'official' voice of national radio and television, most noticeably at first in more popular contexts, such as on Radio 1 and in commercial television advertisements. RP is hardly ever heard in commercials these days. Before long, regional voices began to present other channels, and are now routine, illustrated by the Welsh accent of Huw Edwards reading the news. Non-indigenous accents, especially from the West Indies, began to be heard. Old attitudes die hard, of course, and there will still be those who mourn the passing of the days when a single accent ruled the British airwaves. But they are a steadily shrinking minority.

RP continues to have a strong presence in public broadcasting, but its phonetic character has changed. Accents never stand still, and indeed radio is the chief medium where accent change can be traced. Anyone listening to radio programmes made in the 1920s and 30s can't fail to be struck by the 'plummy' or 'far back' sound of the RP accent then – when, for example, *lord* sounded more like 'lahd' – but even the accents of the 1960s and 70s sound dated now. And changes continue to affect RP. Phoneticians have compared the voice of Queen Elizabeth, as heard in a speech for the opening of parliament, with the voices of Prince Harry or Prince William, two generations on. There are several differences. The Queen would never, for example, replace the final consonant in such words as *hot* with a glottal stop; the youngsters often do. Nor would she use the central vowel quality heard in *the* in such words as *cup*; her version is articulated much further forward in the mouth, more in the direction of *cap*.

Probably the most noticeable accent change has been in relation to what has been called 'Estuary English'. How that came about is a separate question (see **32**).

> The new name (in the 1990s) appealed to the media, and was widely used, though often with uncertainty. Thirty years on, its evolution is much clearer.

'Estuary English' is a variety which attracted media attention in the early 1990s, though the phenomenon had been evolving over many years. The estuary in question was that of the River Thames, and the people who were noticed as having an Estuary accent lived on either side of it. Phonetically it can be roughly placed as an accent intermediate between Received Pronunciation (RP) and London Cockney. Or rather, a range of accents, for Estuary is a broad label, covering several closely related ways of speaking.

Features of Estuary radiated from the London area to other parts of the country. They didn't replace the local accents of these areas; rather they modified the phonetic character of those accents, pulling the vowels and consonants in different directions. The Estuary now heard in Hampshire is very different from that heard in Leicestershire. But in all places, old-timers in a rural village today sound very different from the younger generations who live there. It's this proliferation of accents which is the national pattern. People sometimes claim that 'accents are dying out'. What they've noticed is the disappearance of old rural ways of speech as the people who used them pass away. But the people who now live in these localities still have accents, though very different in character.

When an RP speaker is influenced by a regional accent, or vice versa, the result has been called 'modified RP', and we hear modified Scouse (in Liverpool), modified Glaswegian, modified everything these days. I myself am a heavily modified speaker, using an accent which is a mixture of my original North Wales (where I now live), Liverpool (where I spent my secondary school years), and the south of England (where I worked for twenty years). Apart from the overall auditory impression of my accent, which is difficult to 'place', it displays certain features characteristic of all modified accents, such as inconsistency – for instance, I sometimes say *example* and *bath* with a 'short *a*', and sometimes with a 'long *a*' (*exahmple*, *bahth*). And because I accommodate to my (now grown-up) children, who have been influenced by a more recent set of trends (such as American English), I sometimes say *schedule* with a *sh-* and sometimes with a *sk-*. There are many such variant forms in my speech, and, these days, mixed-accent speakers like me are in the majority.

Mixed accents are especially noticeable in the major population centres of the country, where we hear a remarkable increase in the range of accents, brought about largely by the influx of people of diverse ethnic origin. In Liverpool, there used to be only 'Scouse'; today we can hear Chinese Scouse, Jamaican Scouse, and an array of accent mixes reflecting the growing cosmopolitan character of that city. London, of course, is where this trend is most noticeable. There are many ethnically influenced Estuary accents there now.

Why did Estuary spread so widely and so rapidly? It's the result of two complementary trends. First, an improved standard of living for many people formerly living in London's East End allowed them to move 'up-market' into the outer suburbs and the townships of the home counties, such as Essex, Kent and Hertfordshire. As they began to interact with their new neighbours, their accents naturally accommodated to them, adopting local features of speech (including some RP). At the same time, people from counties further afield were commuting to London in increasing numbers, their travel facilitated by the new motorway system and faster rail connections. With cities such as Hull, Leeds, Manchester and Bristol now only a couple of hours away, huge numbers of people arrived in London with regional accents and found themselves accommodating to the accents of the city. It was now the commuters who adopted London ways of speaking. And when these commuters returned home, they brought those London features back with them. And thus the accent spread.

33

Why do some people say _after<u>noon</u>_ and some say _<u>af</u>ternoon_?

> The variation here reflects a basic property of English rhythm, and draws our attention to many examples of a similar kind.

Actually this isn't anything to do with variation among people. The same person will use both. The reason is to do with the stress-timed (tum-te-tum-te-tum) nature of English rhythm. People unconsciously switch their pronunciation as they move words about a sentence. We would normally say:

> _I have a <u>mee</u>ting this after<u>noon</u>._
> _I have an <u>af</u>ternoon <u>mee</u>ting._

The change takes place because we find it uncomfortable to put two stressed syllables together:

> _I have an after<u>noon</u> <u>mee</u>ting._

It's not impossible. Some speakers will say it without it feeling odd; but research studies have shown that they are a minority. Most people try to preserve the 'tum-te-tum' pattern, and the faster they speak the more this is likely to happen.

Here are some other examples:

> _<u>There's</u> Heath<u>row</u>._ v _<u>Heath</u>row <u>Air</u>port._
> _That's an ideal <u>choice</u>._ v _<u>That's</u> i<u>deal</u>._
> _This is a picture of <u>Princess</u> <u>Mary</u>._ v _A <u>fine</u> prin<u>cess</u>._
> _I'll order some <u>Chinese</u> <u>food</u>._ v _We'll <u>eat</u> Chi<u>nese</u>._
> _The house has an outside <u>loo</u>._ v _It's <u>cold</u> out<u>side</u>._
> _I <u>like</u> Aberdeen._ v _The beef is <u>Aber</u>deen <u>An</u>gus._
> _I have <u>six</u>teen <u>pages</u> to read._ v _He's six<u>teen</u>._

This last is a very productive pattern, as it applies to all _-teen_ numerals, as well as to compounds – _thirty-three, forty-one_ ...

> _I have <u>forty</u>-five pages to read._
> _How old is he? Forty-<u>five</u>._

In technical studies of English phonology, you will come across the term 'the thirteen men rule' referring to this kind of stress shift.

Interestingly, in contexts of contrastive stress, you will occasionally hear a suffix becoming the focus of the contrast. Normally we'd expect:

> Masaki is *Japanese not Chinese.*

This is because pronunciation parallelism is an expected feature when drawing a contrast. But the other day I heard:

> Masaki is *Japanese not Chinese.*

Unusual, but evidently possible for some people.

There are also regional variations in stress. Scottish and Irish English have many examples where the stress is placed later in the word, as in *realize* and *educate*. And poetry is likely to do strange things to stress, and exactly the same kind of stress shift can be seen in a poem with a rigid metre, such as a limerick:

> There was an old groom of Siberia
> Who was once diagnosed with diphtheria
> But when isolated
> And his horse confiscated
> He fell into a state of hysteria.

The words ending the third and fourth lines could not be said in any other way, with the stress on *-ated*, whatever your dialect background.

Stress shift is also one of the most noticeable differences between American and British pronunciation. Compare these pairs:

British	*address ballet cafe donate frontier garage magazine premier research translate weekend*
American	*address ballet cafe donate frontier garage magazine premier research translate weekend*

Because British pronunciation has for some time been influenced by American, any of the above might be heard in Britain these days, especially among young people. For the generation that grew up watching episodes of *Star Trek*, there is only one way to pronounce *frontier*, and that is as in 'Space: the Final Frontier'.

34

Why do people drop the final g when they say *good morning*?

This is a lovely illustration of how social history plays such an important part in the study of pronunciation.

It's not really a /g/, of course. The final consonant shown by the spelling *ng* is a nasal consonant, written as /ŋ/ in the International Phonetic Alphabet. In *mornin'* this has been replaced by /n/. The usage has a long history, heard in any final unstressed syllable, as in *nothin'*, and especially in the *-ing* ending of verbs (as in *runnin'*). It's virtually obligatory in popular music, and may even be seen in titles, such as *Blowin' in the Wind* and *You've Lost that Lovin' Feelin'*. It wouldn't happen in a stressed syllable: *spring* is never heard as *sprin'* or *among* as *amon'*. Because people know how the words should be spelled, they talk about 'dropping the g', though in fact no /g/ sound has been dropped at all.

Once the *-ing* spelling became established, people who had learned to read and write began to insist on the pronunciation reflecting it. By 1800 /ŋ/ was the only acceptable form. John Walker, the compiler of the first *English Pronouncing Dictionary* (1791), demands it, and during the 19th century it became the educated norm, with /n/ a sign of 'vulgar' speech. In 19th-century novels, one of the signs that speakers are lower-class is that we see the *g*'s dropped in spelling. Probably the most famous example (you will find it in books of quotations) is in Charles Dickens' *David Copperfield*, Chapter 8, where Barkis the carrier makes a marriage proposal to Peggotty in the words *Barkis is willin'*.

The opposite effect also happened. Lower-class characters, sensing that there was something 'upper class' about the use of /ŋ/, began to over-use it, replacing /n/ in words that never had an /ŋ/ in their history, saying *captain* as *capting* and *garden* as *garding*. (Linguists call this sort of thing *hypercorrection* – when a speaker goes beyond the norm of a target variety because of a desire to be correct.)

The situation might have stayed that way, with /ŋ/ being the educated norm and /n/ considered vulgar. But during the 19th century something very unusual took place: the very top end of society also began to drop their *g*'s. It was a practice that generated a catchphrase describing aristocratic users: those who went *huntin', shootin' and fishin'*. This pronunciation lasted well into the 20th century, and even though it's little heard today, the memory of past usage is still there.

Why did this happen? I think it was because during the late 18th century people became increasingly self-conscious about language. The period saw the rise of the prescriptive approach to language, the growth of the elocution movement, and the publication of the first dictionaries and manuals of pronunciation. These were intended to show the new and aspiring middle class, anxious to avoid criticism from upper-class polite society, how to speak 'correctly'. There were no such anxieties, of course, if you were a member of the upper class. The new rule books were not for them. So, if the lower classes were being schooled in the use of /ŋ/ as the everyday pronunciation of *-ing*, then upper-class usage would show its superiority by doing the opposite. Hence, huntin', shootin', fishin'.

G-dropping is less socially divisive in the UK today. It's still commonly heard in regional accents, but people who speak in Received Pronunciation can also replace /ŋ/. It depends on the level of formality. In formal speech, or when reading aloud, they're likely to keep /ŋ/; but in informal speech it's very often replaced by /n/. Some words are likely to make the replacement more than others: for example, the colloquial pronunciation of *going to* is so common that it has developed an accepted spelling *gonna*. And even the most fastidious RP /ŋ/-user will occasionally offer someone a cheery colloquial g-dropped greeting: *Mornin'!, Evenin' all!*

35 Why am I hearing so many high rising tones on statements these days?

This feature of intonation has attracted most public attention in recent years. Where did it come from?

It's an accurate impression. The phenomenon has even been given its own label: *uptalk*. And it's one of the features of contemporary speech in the younger generation that has attracted most condemnation by older British people who claim they would never use it.

The phenomenon began to be noticed in the UK during the 1980s, associated chiefly with young New Zealanders and Australians, and was transmitted to a wider audience through the Australian soap *Neighbours*. At the same time, an American version, associated initially with young Californians, was being widely encountered through films and television. At first, frequent usage was largely among young women, but it soon spread to young men, and has since been working its way up the age-range.

Its value lies in its succinctness: it allows someone to make a statement and ask a question at the same time. If I say, 'I've just seen Godot?', with a high rising tone on the name, the intonation acts as an unspoken question. ('Do you know the play?') If you do, you'll simply nod and let me continue. If you don't, my intonation offers you a chance to get clarification. I don't have to spell out the options. ('Do you know the play or don't you?') It's also a convenient way of establishing rapport, as the intonation offers the other participants the chance to intervene.

Uptalk also has an important social role. If I use it, I'm assuming that you do know what I'm talking about, so we must know each other well enough. If I say, 'I saw Jean the other day', with a high rising tone on *Jean*, the implication is: 'Of course you know who Jean is, because we're mates'. The usage is thus likely to be heard among those who have a shared social background. That's probably the main reason it caught on so much among teenagers: it affirmed mutual recognition as members of a circle.

In fact, uptalk isn't as new as people think. Several British regional accents have long been associated with a rising lilt on statements, especially in the Celtic fringe. I live in Wales and hear it around me all the time. That's probably the main reason people call the accent 'musical'. And I suspect that's how uptalk got into the antipodes in the first place, travelling with the early settlers. But it's by no means restricted to people with a Celtic background. It can turn up in the speech of anyone – though not with the frequency with which it's used by the younger generation.

There is a very early indication of its presence in British English in Joshua Steele's essay on *The Melody and Measure of Speech* (1775). He was the first to transcribe intonational patterns using a musical notation, and he noticed it (and evidently didn't like it). He mentions '... how much the voice is let down in the conclusion of periods, with respect both to loudness and tone, according to the practice of the best speakers,' and adds, 'I have observed, that many speakers offend in this article; some keeping up their ends too high.'

Like it or not, statements spoken in a questioning way are part of English, so the intention behind them needs to be shown through punctuation if we want to reflect this kind of mutually affirming dialogue in our writing. We're less likely to find question marks at the end of statements in written monologues or formal conversations; but they do occur in places where informality is the norm, as in these 2020 tweets:

We need to send this to their marketing people?
This is the best thing he's done since the O2 concert?

We can imagine the rising tones as these sentences reach their close. At the beginning the writers seem definite, but they are asking for reassurance from their mates at the end. And 'mates' here means the entire Twitter community!

D: Spelling and punctuation

Questions about individual words and grammatical constructions, by their nature, are sporadic: they vary from one sentence to the next. But spelling and punctuation are always in front of our eyes, so variation and change is very noticeable, and prompt many questions about usage.

36　Why is English spelling so irregular?

37　Why is *encyclopaedia* sometimes spelled *encyclopedia*?

38　Why do we see a verb sometimes spelled with *-ise* and sometimes with *-ize?*

39　Should I write words with accents, like *cliché* and *naïve?*

40　Should I write *Past Perfect* or *past perfect* (and for other names of tenses)?

41　Why is there so much variation in the use of the apostrophe?

42　I've seen both *red, white and blue* and *red, white, and blue.* Which should I use?

43　Can I use an exclamation mark along with a question mark to add emphasis to a question, as in *What?!* or *What!?*

44　Are hyphens going out of fashion?

If you're reading this easily, you've managed to decode English spelling, despite its irregularities. But where did the oddities come from? There's a story behind every word.

Why *hiccough* and not *hiccup*?
It was actually written in such forms as *hikup* and *hickup* when it arrived in English in the 16th century. But a popular feeling arose that there was a connection with a cough. So, people reasoned, if *cough* was spelled with *ough*, *hiccough* should be the same. But the earlier pronunciation stayed.

Why *love* and not *luv*?
The word was actually spelled with a *u* in Anglo-Saxon times. But when the French scribes wrote it down, they found it difficult to read, because the letters *u* and *v* looked the same. So they changed the 'u' vowel to an 'o'.

Why *debt* and not *det*?
When the word arrived in English in the 13th century, it was spelled *det*, *dett*, *dette*, and suchlike. But spelling reformers decided that a single spelling was desirable, so to help fix one in people's minds, they looked to Latin, where the word was *debitum*, and added a silent 'b'. They thought it would help!

Why *scorn* and *skin* and not *skorn* and *scin*?
It depends on the language the words came from. Words that came into English from French, Latin, and Greek usually end up with *sc*, as in *scorn* and *scarce*. Words from Old Norse or Dutch keep the spelling used in those languages, as in *skin* and *skipper*.

Why *dance* and not *dans*?
Because the French scribes liked to spell words ending in an 's' sound with *ce*. In Old English, *mice* was spelled *mys*, but it changed to its modern form in the Middle Ages. We see that French preference in many words, such as *since*, *fence* and *face*.

Why *lamb* and not *lam*?
In Old English, the final *b* was pronounced in such words as *lamb*, *dumb* and *climb*. Because *m* and *b* are both made with the two lips, after a while people didn't bother pronouncing the *b*. But people had got used to the earlier spelling, so it stayed.

Why *ghost* and not *gost*?
The word was spelled *gost* originally. But when William Caxton began to print books in England in the 15th century, his Flemish typesetters didn't know English very well, so they spelled several words in a Flemish way, and *ghost* was one of those which caught on. It was reinforced by its use in the English translations of the Bible a century later, where we find the Father, Son and *Holy Ghost*, not *Holy Gost*.

Why *queen* and not *kween* or *cween*?
It was spelled with a *c* originally in Old English: *cwen*, with a long *e*, and sometimes, in later manuscripts, *kwen*. But evidently French scribes didn't like this spelling, and replaced it with one of their favourite letters, *q* – still a notable feature of French orthography. From the 13th century, we find both *queen* and *qween*, but the latter died out during the Middle English period.

Why *strudel* and not *stroodle*?
When German *Nudel* arrived in English in the late 18th century it was immediately spelled *noodle*, following the common -*dle* ending, as in *puddle*, *doodle* and *saddle*; but a century later *Strudel* came into English and kept its original spelling. This is because people had begun to respect exotic spellings – something we still do today. We write *ciao* and not *chow*.

When you read stories like these, you can see some of the reasons for spelling irregularity. From an original fairly phonetic system (Old English), waves of new influences on writing – French, Dutch, and later Latin and Greek – added new conventions, and these, along with new ways of thinking about spelling, resulted in the present-day situation. But don't overstate the problem. The original phonetic system is still there, and works well most of the time.

Why is *encyclopaedia* sometimes spelled *encyclopedia*?

37

> There's more variation in English spelling today than
> people realize.

If you go to a general-purpose dictionary, you'll find on average about
three variant forms on each page. In the early pages of letter *A* we will
find *absinthe* and *absinth*, *adieus* and *adieux*, *adrenalin* and *adrenaline*,
and many more. There may even be three variants (such as *aerie, aery,
erie*) or four (*anaesthetise, anaesthetize, anesthetise, anesthetize*). In one
study, the variants amounted to around six percent of all words. In a
scientific or technical dictionary that figure is going to be much greater,
because many words use a suffix such as *-in/-ine* or a prefix such as
paedo-/pedo- or *archae-/arche-*. In specialized dictionaries it rises to
around 14 percent.

The increase is partly due to differences between American and British
English, with the former increasingly influencing the latter. That's why
we find the two spellings of *encyclop(a)edia*: the traditional British
spelling was *ae*, and the American spelling *e*, and the latter has spread.
My encyclopedias for Cambridge were all spelled with an *e* – so when
the oldest publishing house in the world adopts such a spelling, we can
be sure it's a major trend.

But not all variation can be explained by American influence. Some
variants reflect different intuitions over which of two spellings better
represents the content of a specialism. For example, we're more likely
to find the conservative *ae* spelling in subjects which have historical
content. In a Google search in 2020, the 'modern' subject of *pediatrics*
was eight times more frequent than *paediatrics*, and *etiology* was
four times more frequent than *aetiology*; but the 'historical' subject of
archaeology was seven times more frequent than *archeology*.

Academic tradition is also an important factor. Most people write
taboo, but if we see *tabu*, then we're probably reading something by an
anthropologist. In British English, most people write *programme*, unless

they're in the world of computing, in which case it's *program*. Most people vary between *judgement* and *judgment*, but judges making a decision always use *judgment*.

Food words from other cultures are especially varied. Look at the menu in different Indian restaurants, and you'll see *popadoms, poppadums, popadums, papadoms, poppodoms, poppadams*, and more. And we eat *yoghurt, yogurt, yogourt* or *yoghourt* as well as *hummus, houmous, hummos, hummous* or *humus*. All lexicographers can do here is note the variants and hope that eventually one form will emerge triumphant.

An old spelling can help show the character of a variety of English, such as legal language (*shew* for *showed*) or religious language (*alway* for *always*). And a specific tradition can motivate exceptional spellings. *Crucifixion* is a good example of a word which has retained a spelling in a religious setting which, when compared with other uses of this word-ending, is impossible (*detection*, never *detexion*) or archaic (*connexion*): it ought to be *crucifiction* (compare *fiction*), but the influence of Latin (*crucifixus*) introduced the *x* for *crucifix* in the 15th century and it became the norm in Christianity. Cultural preferences may also motivate the use of a particular spelling, such as to show a political or religious identity (*Québec* v *Quebec, Muslim* v *Moslem*).

The percentage of spelling variation rises again if we include in our notion of spelling other phenomena than the selection and ordering of letters. There are many variations in capitalization, for example (see **40**): is it *moon* or *Moon, president* or *President*? There are variations in spacing and hyphenation: is it *flower pot, flower-pot* or *flowerpot*? *No one, no-one* or *noone*? *E-mail* or *email*? And if we add the transliteration of proper names from other languages to our list, it rises still further. *Tschaikovsky, Tchaikovsky, Tschaikofsky, Tchaikofsky* ...? *Tutankhamen, Tutankhamun, Tut'ankhamun* ...? If we include absolutely everything, the variation level rises to around 20 percent.

What to do? Publishers choose one form in their house styles and stick to it. All we can do is follow their example. A consistent spelling policy in a school is a great help.

Why do we see a verb sometimes spelled with -*ise* and sometimes with -*ize*?

38

This is one of the most frequently encountered variations in English spelling. The reasons lie deep within the history of the language.

The -*ize* spelling was preferred by classical scholars, especially in the 16th century, for verbs with that ending which came into English from Greek and Latin, where *z* was used, and that etymological argument has fostered the use of *z* ever since. Dr Johnson's *Dictionary*, published in 1755, has *agonize, analyze, anatomize* and so on, and this was hugely influential. The USA and Canada adopted it from the outset. And John Murray, the editor of the major new dictionary project at the end of the 19th century – what would eventually become the *Oxford English Dictionary* – opted for it too, partly influenced by Johnson, and also on phonological grounds, noting that the letter *z* better reflects the sound. At the turn of the century, Henry Hart compiled his 'Rules for Compositors and Readers' at the press in Oxford. He opens his first booklet with a section on spellings, and adopts the -*ize* spellings used in Murray's dictionary.

So where did the -*ise* alternative come from? Some of the words, such as the verb related to *baptism*, were spelled with both an *s* and a *z* from their earliest days in Middle English: *baptise, baptize*. The trend to spell with *s* began when verbs came into English with increasing frequency from French, where the suffix was -*iser*. The thinking was still etymological. A verb of this kind borrowed directly from French, it was argued, should be spelled with -*ise*, to reflect that source. An additional argument was that the *s* would reinforce a spelling link between related words, such as *analyse* and *analyst, terrorise* and *terrorism, televise* and *television*. And during the 19th century, this usage grew.

The problem, of course, is that it's often unclear whether a verb has come into English from French or from Latin. We're not so conscious of etymology these days as dictionary users were once expected to be. Confusion led printers to try to sort it out, and they did this by imposing a uniform rule for all such verbs where alternatives exist. Hart, as I've said, opted for *-ize*. But several other publishers – perhaps in an effort to distinguish themselves from Oxford – decided to use *-ise*. They may also have been influenced by the fact that there are fewer exceptions if you go for the *-ise* rule. Several verbs traditionally appear only with *-ise*, and you have to remember what they are (see below).

World usage varies. The overall preference in North America is for *-ize*; in Australia, *-ise*. In the UK *-ise* currently beats *-ize* in a ratio of 3:2. But usage is always divided – and is changing. Verbs that were once only *-ise* are now sometimes seen with *-ize*, such as *advertize*, despite dictionary recommendations. Publishers may allow either, though of course insisting on consistency within a single work. The issue is frequently in front of our eyes, as derived nouns and adjectives also present the problem, as in *organis/zation* and *recognis/zable*. The process is open-ended, because verbs can always be formed from names of people or places in the sense of 'act like, be in the character of', as in *Americanis/ze* and *Bowdleris/ze*. There are lots of nonce usages. I recently heard someone say, after living in the capital for a while, that he had been thoroughly *Londonis/zed*.

If you're writing something for publication, therefore, the publisher will probably make the decision for you. In private writing, it's up to you – but, whichever spelling you decide to use, it's stylistically elegant to be consistent. Personally, having had my usage pushed first one way and then the other by publishers over the years, I've given up having a preference!

Some common *ise*-only verbs
advertise, advise, apprise, arise, chastise, circumcise, comprise, compromise, despise, devise, disguise, enterprise, exercise, excise, exercise, franchise, improvise, prise, revise, supervise, surmise, surprise, televise

Should I write words with accents, like *cliché* and *naïve?*

39

> The general impression is that the use of accent marks is decreasing; but there's one area where they are on the increase.

There's a lot of usage variation these days. The technical term for any mark added to a letter to distinguish it from others is *diacritic,* and English words have used several of them.

- an acute accent, as in *cliché*
- a grave accent, as in *learnèd,* in its sense of 'scholarly'
- a circumflex accent, as in *fête*
- a cedilla, as in *façade*
- a tilde, as in *señor*
- a diaeresis (US dieresis), as in *naïve*

They were first introduced in unfamiliar loanwords as an aid to reading. In some cases they remind people that a vowel has to be sounded. A final *e* in words like *same* and *home* is silent, showing that the preceding vowel is long – compare *same* and *Sam.* So in *cliché* the accent shows that the pronunciation is 'klee-shay' and not 'kleesh'. *Learned* looks like the monosyllabic past tense of *learn*, but as an adjective meaning 'scholarly' it has two syllables, shown by the accent.

The earliest known reference to *diaeresis* is 1611, where it's used to distinguish adjacent vowels in such words as *queuë* – the intention being to ensure that the vowel sequence was not pronounced as a diphthong. This was the reverse of later usage, where it shows that the second vowel *is* to be pronounced separately, as in *naïve,* as well as in proper names, such as *Noël, Zoë* and *the Brontës.* It became very popular during the 18th and 19th centuries with a vowel-distinguishing function, as in *coöperate, reëducate.* Some of the early usages have now died out. Nobody writes *poëm* anymore. And in proper names, the usage is now so uncommon that people have to point it out – 'My name's Chloë with two dots'.

Why has usage reduced? There are several reasons:

- The words have become more familiar. Few nowadays have difficulty recognizing *cliche*, without an accent. Only cases of real ambiguity would warrant a diacritic, as with *learnèd*, to distinguish *learnèd behaviour* (= scholarly) from *learned behaviour* (= acquired).
- In the late 20th century, diacritics didn't suit the graphic fashion to 'declutter' print – the same trend that led to the omission of periods in abbreviations (*B.B.C.* becoming *BBC*).
- The symbols aren't easy to find on an English-language keyboard, so people do without them.
- In the case of the diaeresis, an alternative spelling took over – the hyphen, as in *co-operate* and *re-educate*. But even this is optional: we often now see *cooperate, reeducate,* and the like.

Certainly, if any modern book used accents frequently, it would have to be there for a stylistic reason, such as in representations of regional dialect or alien speech in sci-fi languages.

But there's one context where diacritics are on the increase: in brand names, where it is a purely graphic feature, with little or no effect on pronunciation. The diaeresis especially is having a revival. Some companies, such as *Möben*, *Gü* and *Häagen-Dazs*, have used it to add a Germanic connotation to their names, and sometimes carry the practice over into the words in their advertising copy. And it's become very popular in the names of heavy metal and hard rock groups, as in *Blue Öyster Cult*, *Motörhead* and *The Accüsed*, presumably in an attempt to convey an imagined Wagnerian boldness and ferocity. Over fifty groups have used this 'metal umlaut', as it's called, and it also turns up in some video-game titles, such as *Brütal Legend*.

Dictionary writers don't know what to do! The *Oxford English Dictionary* shows only *cliché* as its headword (in 2020), though an accentless *cliche* is there in some citations, and since the 1920s occurs many times more frequently (as shown by Google's Ngram Viewer). *Learned* is shown only without the accent, though I see it accented often enough in print (including my own writing). So you can write either – but be consistent.

Should I write *Past Perfect* or *past perfect* (and for other names of tenses)?

40

> Nothing seems more straightforward than the contrast between a capital letter and its lower-case partner; but the distinction is not so simple.

The typical semantic function of a capital letter is to draw attention to an item of special significance, such as a proper name or personification, or to Make An Important Comment. Usage variation arises because people will have different views about what is 'specially significant'. In an ELT context, I can easily imagine teachers seeing tense forms as being so important that they feel the need to give them special graphic prominence. But not everyone will see them in this way. Personally, I wouldn't capitalize – nor, I see, does Scott Thornbury in his *101 Grammar Questions* in this series. Tense forms are so frequently mentioned in a grammar book that the capital letters would turn up all over the place, reducing their attention-drawing function, as well as adding to the visual clutter of the page. It is a slippery slope. Present Progressive ... Third Person Singular Present Progressive ... .

Capitalization is a highly variable matter, influenced by personal taste, graphic aesthetics and social trends, so there's never a hard-and-fast rule for examples like these. There is gradience, from the clear-cut case where we're talking about a unique person, place, or thing, to cases where we're talking about a class of entities. Thus, we have *President Trump*, at one extreme, and *The country is governed by a president*, at the other. But there are many intermediate cases.

No simple principle will work for all instances. 'All official titles should be capitalized,' says one house style manual on my shelves. But does this work?

> *He became Emperor of Rome.*
> *He became Emperor of all lands west of ...*
> *He was crowned Emperor.*
> *He acted as Emperor between ...*

The less specific the reference, the more obtrusive becomes the capital letter.

The same point applies to subject areas. Is it: 'There'll be exams in History and Geography' or '... history and geography'? The subject name will have a capital, whereas the generic concept won't. A capital would be obligatory when talking about a specific notion, such as a course or exam paper, e.g. *History 231*, or the name of a department or category. We would need it for *You'll find History on the third floor* (i.e. the department) or *You'll find History in the library* (i.e. the subject) – but not here: *You'll make history in the library* (by doing something dramatic).

Some subject areas have their own conventions. Religious texts may capitalize pronouns referring to divine beings, so that *Jesus*, for example, is referred to as *He*. In specific philosophical contexts we may see certain concepts capitalized, such as *Reason* or *Truth*, to distinguish them from the everyday sense. General usage has examples too: *catholic* v *Catholic*, *a moon* v *the Moon*, *cancer* v *Cancer*. There's even a technical term for words that are capitalized to distinguish a special meaning: *capitonyms*.

Fashion always rules. For the past few years there's been a noticeable trend towards graphical simplicity – *B.B.C.* becoming *BBC*, and the like – and capitals have been affected. You'll find far more in the newspapers of a few decades ago; and in the late 17th and early 18th century most nouns would be capitalized, regardless of whether they were proper names or not. Today, where there is an option, as in subject names, the trend has been to avoid caps. This is the advice of the main copy-editing style guides, and usage generally concurs, at present. 'If in doubt, don't capitalize.' But above all: 'Be consistent, whatever you decide to do.'

And always be prepared for the individual who breaks the rules for special effect, such as A. A. Milne in his 'Winnie the Pooh' stories, talking about Owl and Rabbit:

> Owl hasn't exactly got Brain, but he Knows Things. He would know the Right Thing to Do when Surrounded by Water. There's Rabbit. He hasn't Learnt in Books, but he can always Think of a Clever Plan ...

Why is there so much variation in the use of the apostrophe?

41

No aspect of English usage gets more publicity than the way the apostrophe is used today. To see why, we need to delve into the history of the language.

This question was prompted by a teacher who was travelling on the London Underground. She saw *Earl's Court*, with an apostrophe, and the very next station, *Barons Court*, without one. To see why, we have to explore the history of English.

The apostrophe arrived very late, compared with most other punctuation marks, in the closing decades of the 16th century, and took a long time to develop its present range of standard usage. Grammarians and printers were still trying to work out what the rules were even at the end of the 19th century. They weren't entirely successful, leaving a number of unresolved issues over usage that generated further variation and associated controversy.

Its origins lie in Europe, where 16th-century printers introduced it (based on Greek practice) to show the omission of a letter (usually, a vowel). They then began to use it to mark possession, but in a very erratic way. We see far more examples of possessives lacking an apostrophe than showing one. There may be vacillation even in a single line: *Did Romeo's hand shed Tybalts blood* is found in Shakespeare's First Folio. Eventually the notion grew that 'apostrophe = possession', not only in nouns but also in pronouns: we see such spellings as *her's*, *our's*, and *it's*. But people also used it to mark a plural, especially of foreign words ending in a vowel, such as *agenda's* and *folio's*.

In the 17th century, practice slowly standardized. The use of an apostrophe to mark a possessive extended to all nouns. Printers later developed the rules which made the distinction between singular and plural possession (*cat's* v *cats'*) – though not entirely consistently, as they decided not to use one in possessive pronouns. So today we have to write *the dog's bowl*, but *its bowl* and *it is hers*. The uncertainty about how to use the apostrophe increased.

This soon affected proper names. In the 19th century, there was huge debate over shop names: is it *Harrod's* or *Harrods*? Inconsistency was the result, in all walks of life – including the Underground. So today we find *Earl's Court* for the station, but local street names are spelled *Earls*. *Barons Court* never had an apostrophe. There are lots of puzzles like this: you go to *Shepherd's Bush* tube station to visit *Shepherds Bush Market*.

The 20th-century design fashion to 'declutter' public signs led to many apostrophes being omitted, reinforced by the trend to omit them on the internet, especially in contracted forms (*dont*, *isnt*, etc.). *King's Cross* station keeps its apostrophe, but go online to National Rail Enquiries (and many other sites) and you will see *Kings Cross*.

Another factor promoting uncertainty is that the practice of using one to mark a plural never totally died away, as can be seen in contemporary spellings such as *the 1980's*. Abbreviations also often use it, especially if there's a possibility of confusion with some other word, as in these examples:

- *A's, B's and Rarities* (record album name), where *As* would be confusing
- *Don't forget to dot the i's and cross the t's* (meaning to pay close attention to detail when completing a task), where *dot the is* would be confusing
- *The pro's and con's*, where *pros* might not be recognized or be mispronounced (as 'pross').

The centuries-old feeling that we need to separate a word ending in a vowel from the *s* is still widespread, which is why words like *banana* and *tomato* attract it (thus motivating its dismissive label as 'the greengrocer's apostrophe'). This of course is an error in Standard English, and some people take delight in going around with a marker pen and correcting the spelling whenever they see it. But if you decide to do this, beware! A few years ago, two Americans ended up in court when they corrected an apostrophe error in a heritage site sign. They were landed with a huge fine and only narrowly avoided going to jail.

I've seen both *red, white and blue* and *red, white, and blue*. Which should I use?

42

> This is a serious competitor for the title of 'most contentious topic in English punctuation' (a title currently held by the subject of the previous chapter).

This is another area where usage is seriously divided, and the option you go for will depend on which publisher you read or which style guide you want to follow. The history of the controversy over what is called 'the serial comma' explains what happened.

The first English grammarians, both in Britain and the USA, all used the comma. And when Horace Hart devised the printing-house rules for Oxford University Press in 1893 he recommended it. This is the relevant section:

> where more than two words or phrases occur together in a sequence a comma should precede the final *and*; e.g. A great, wise, and beneficient measure.

Generations of writers have followed his lead and called the usage 'the Oxford comma'.

What was his reasoning? An earlier writer, David Steel, explained it this way in his *Elements of Punctuation* (1786). He took the sentence *Ulysses was a wise, eloquent, cautious, and intrepid hero* and gives this explanation: '*intrepid* is not more particularly connected with *hero* than *wise* or *eloquent* – all equally belong to the substantive, and ought to have the same degree of separation or connection'.

So there's a solid semantic reason why the comma should be there: it reinforces the parallelism between all the items in a list. If we leave it out, that sense of connectivity is reduced – though in examples like the *Ulysses* sentence not by much. That's why people began to omit it: they argue that it makes no difference to the meaning, and that *and* does the connecting job of the comma anyway, as shown by such alternatives as *an old, comfortable chair* and *an old and comfortable chair*. This comma does 'no useful work' said Eric Partridge in his book on punctuation, *You Have a Point There* (1953).

The omission grew gradually during the early 20th century. Newspapers and magazines on the whole avoided it, to save space and (in the days when typesetting was painstakingly by hand) time and energy. Critics argued that an unnecessary comma was an intrusion that delayed the reader. And developing a clean look to the page was one of the ways in which a forward-looking publishing house could distinguish itself from the conservative practices of other presses. That presumably is why Cambridge University Press, anxious to distinguish itself from Oxford, routinely abandoned it.

But as the century progressed, some publishers began to take a more equable view, acknowledging the fact that diversity was the norm. Judith Butcher, in her influential handbook for Cambridge University Press, *Copy-editing*, allows both practices:

> In lists of three or more items, a comma should be consistently omitted or included before the final 'and': red, white and blue; red, white, and blue.

The important word was *consistently*. And whichever school you belonged to, everyone agreed that there were exceptions, and that avoidance of ambiguity must be the primary rule. If it's ambiguous to omit the comma, don't omit it. If it's ambiguous to insert the comma, don't insert it. Take a sentence like this one:

> *I've invited two friends, my agent and my publisher.*
> *I've invited two friends, my agent, and my publisher.*

How many people are being invited? Two or four? Omitting the comma suggests two; inserting the comma suggests four.

There'd be less chance of ambiguity in speech, because the intonation would point the difference. The first sentence would very likely be said with a falling tone on *friends* and a following brief pause; *my agent* and *my publisher* would then be linked rhythmically as a single intonation unit. In the second, *friends* would have a rising tone, as would *agent*, and the intonation would be spread equally over the three items.

Can I use an exclamation mark along with a question mark, as in *What?!* or *What!?*

43

> This is a good example of how personal taste and changes in fashion are never far away when dealing with questions of punctuation.

The implication is that the questioner has been told off for doing so. And indeed, there has been antagonism towards the use of the exclamation mark for a long time, and especially since the 19th century, when writers used it a great deal, especially in the more lurid novels of the time. Henry Fowler, in his *Dictionary of Modern English Usage* (1926), condemns the 'excessive use of exclamation marks [as] one of the things that betray the uneducated or unpractised writer', and elsewhere he adds that it shows the kind of writer 'who wants to add a spurious dash of sensation to something unsensational'.

So the use of an exclamation mark along with the question mark attracted even extra condemnation from stylists, and 20th-century house styles generally recommended the removal of exclamation marks unless absolutely necessary. Copy-editors would never allow a multiple mark (!!, !!!), except in such genres as novels and poetry where the author insisted – and even then, they would do their best to persuade the author to remove them.

But this prescriptive trend hasn't stopped their use, and in settings where copy-editors are absent, we see multiple forms frequently, especially in online genres where emotional expression is not being artificially constrained. Indeed, on the internet there's been a remarkable proliferation of uses, including emails in which exclamation and question marks are combined in long sequences (?!?!?!) and used idiosyncratically along with other forms (such as ?!**!?, which I received in an email recently, and which I interpreted as an emphatic questioning explosion of some sort). There has even been an institutionalization of the basic combination, in the form of the *interrobang* (‽), which is now recognized by the organization that established graphical computing standards, Unicode; but you'll not often see it because it's missing from keyboards.

It isn't just the internet, however. The combined form makes available a further semantic distinction in any informal context:

- *Why on earth would Chris ever want to do such a thing?* – a genuine question
- *Why on earth would Chris ever want to do such a thing!* – an emphatic comment
- *Why on earth would Chris ever want to do such a thing?!* – a genuine question with added emphasis – the question function is primary in the speaker's mind
- *Why on earth would Chris ever want to do such a thing!?* – an emphatic comment with a questioning tone. The question is an afterthought, a bit like:
- *Why on earth would Chris ever want to do such a thing!* – huh?

If you do decide to become a multiple exclamation mark user, take care, as once you board the exclamation bus, it's difficult to get off. And if you try to, you can easily convey the opposite of what you intended. Imagine the following in a series of messages from Jane:

> *I'm fine!*
> *But you'll never guess what happened!!*
> *I met John again!!!*

If the fourth sentence is 'And he wants to come over,' it will be important to get the punctuation right. Increasing the number of exclamation marks will suggest she is pleased at the prospect:

> *He wants to come over!!!!*

If she reduces them, the prospect seems to be much less exciting:

> *He wants to come over!*

And reverting to a period would make the prospect sound even worse:

> *He wants to come over.*

Most of the time it isn't possible to 'settle' arguments about punctuation, as attitudes are very much bound up with personal taste and trends in fashion. But overuse of any linguistic feature draws attention to itself (as we saw in **17** and **21**), and can distract from the content of the message, so it's usually wise to take the advice of the house styles and use exclamation marks judiciously, especially offline.

Are hyphens going out of fashion?

44

They're still with us, but hugely influenced by changes in fashion and practice.

My questioner had seen *today*, *tonight* and *tomorrow* written with a hyphen: *to-day*, *to-night*, *to-morrow*. He must have been reading a writer such as Charles Dickens or other publications from a century or more ago, when this was normal. The origins of the practice lie in etymology. The three words were originally (in Old and Middle English) a preposition (*to*) followed by a separate word (*dæg*, *niht*, *morwen*). Gradually a sense of their use as single notions developed, so the two elements were brought together in writing, but with considerable variation in usage. In the earliest manuscripts, we find all three possibilities: *tonight*, *to night* and *to-night*.

The view that they should be written as separate words was reinforced when Dr Johnson listed them in his dictionary (1755) under *to* as *to day*, *to morrow* and *to night*. But during the 19th century, dictionaries opted for the hyphen in all three words, and this was further reinforced when dialect scholars included other forms. Joseph Wright, in his *English Dialect Dictionary* (completed in 1906) hyphenates them all, and adds *to-year* (= 'this year', in general dialect use in Britain and Ireland) and *to-morn* (= 'tomorrow', especially in the north of England).

The *Oxford English Dictionary* shows hyphenated examples throughout the 19th century and into the early 20th. The steady disappearance of the hyphenated forms in the 20th was influenced by Henry Fowler, who in his *Dictionary of Modern English Usage* (1926) comes out against it: 'The lingering of the hyphen, which is still usual after the *to* of these words, is a very singular piece of conservatism.' However, the usage was already dying out as he was writing. The last examples of hyphenated forms in the *Oxford English Dictionary* are all from the 1930s, in newspapers and magazines.

But more recent instances of the older usage can still be found. I have personal experience of all three words continuing to be hyphenated as late as the 1970s, as for some years now I've been editing the work of the poet John Bradburne, who died in 1979. In all his writing he consistently hyphenates. But he was a poet very much aware of the past, and one who often used archaisms.

Some other compound time words have shown a similar development. *Weekend*, for example, was additionally *week end* and *week-end* in Victorian times. *Year-end*, however, has retained its hyphen. And we also find instances of *after noon* and *after-noon* alongside *afternoon*. *Nowadays* had even more variants: *now-a-days* and *now a days*, as well as *now o' days*, *now of days* and *now on days*.

English writers have always had an uncertain relationship with the hyphen in compound words. In 2007, about 16,000 previously hyphenated words in the sixth edition of the *Shorter Oxford Dictionary* lost their hyphens. Some, such as *ice-cream*, became 'open' – the two words separated by a space. Others, such as *leap-frog*, became 'closed' – written without a space. Why the change? All the dictionary was doing was trying to keep up with how people were actually using the hyphen in their writing. They examined millions of words of text to discover the patterns. And English users, it seems, often change their minds. On the whole, the modern tendency is to use an open or closed form, rather than a hyphenated one. Perhaps part of a mood to reduce visual clutter? Or is it just that online typists find it easier to do without them? The position of the hyphen on a keyboard doesn't help.

So, to hyphenate or not to hyphenate? Dictionaries are likely to tell you different things, depending on when they were last revised and the data they've collected to inform their thinking. American and British usage is often different. The only advice I can offer is to be consistent with whichever one you choose – and be tolerant of those who choose differently!

E: Genres

The many varieties of English – historical, regional, social, occupational, literary, personal – have been frequently referred to in earlier pages. In this final section, I take a closer look at some of them.

There's a widespread belief that Shakespearean English is a totally different language from Modern English. Some have even argued that he needs to be translated into Modern English before we can understand him. But it's a myth.

The language of Shakespeare's time is often called Elizabethan English, which reinforces the belief that it's very different. A better label is Early Modern English, which stresses the continuity between then and now. There's far more in common between Shakespeare's English and ours than people think.

Shakespeare needs translation? You be the judge, with this example. Romeo has just met Juliet, and they've had a first conversation together, she on the balcony, he in the garden below. They say goodnight, and she goes in, then comes out again.

Juliet: What o'clock tomorrow
        Shall I send to thee?
Romeo: By the hour of nine.
Juliet: I will not fail. 'Tis twenty year till then.
        I have forgot why I did call thee back.

Now that piece of dialogue isn't exactly like Modern English, even though I bet you understood all of it. Some of the phrasing feels old-fashioned. Instead of *What o'clock?* we'd now say *What time? By the hour of nine* would be *By nine. Twenty year* would be *twenty years* in Standard English (though it's still used in many local dialects), as is *I have forgot* for *I have forgotten*. And of course they say *thee* to each other, not *you*, but most learners will recognize what's going on there, because they have a similar intimate/formal distinction in their own languages (as in French *tu/vous*, German *du/Sie*, and so on).

How much of Shakespeare is just like this? When compiling *Shakespeare's Words* (www.shakespeareswords.com) I did some counting in all the plays and poems. The database contains some 46,000 occurrences of words that are different in some way between Shakespeare's day and now. That sounds like a lot, but there are 931,000 words in the entire canon of 39 plays, so it's actually only five percent. You aren't very often going to encounter a word which differs in form or meaning from what exists today – and a similar figure also applies to the grammatical differences.

The reason people think of Shakespeare's language as difficult is because they remember the passages where several of the unfamiliar words cluster together. Such passages do require special study, indeed. Some of the sentences are quite long, too, requiring that we take special care with them. And word order variations caused by the rhythm of the poetic line can also interfere with comprehension. But on the whole, the language is the same, and we can use our Modern English intuitions to follow what is going on well enough. Children do. I've often seen groups of youngsters watch a play at Stratford or in Shakespeare's Globe and laugh, gasp or cry as occasion demanded. They didn't understand every word, but the context (and of course good acting) helped them through the trickier passages.

The crucial point, of course, is that they were watching and listening, not reading. If their first exposure to a play is through a dull-looking textbook with lots of notes, then I'm not at all surprised to find people thinking Shakespeare is difficult. These days it's easy to avoid that dry-as-dust encounter, with so many plays available on film. But you can't beat the shared excitement that comes from seeing and hearing a play along with an audience. Stage before page, always.

46 How has English changed in the last 400 years?

All aspects of language have been affected, as the examples of spelling, punctuation, vocabulary, grammar and pronunciation illustrate.

Spelling will certainly be the most noticeable feature. Old texts, such as Shakespeare's *Sonnets* (1609), are usually published today using modern conventions. The original version looked like this extract from Sonnet 104:

Three beautious springs to yellow Autumne turn'd,
In processe of the seasons haue I seene.
Three Aprill perfumes in three hot Iunes burn'd,
Since first I saw you fresh which yet are greene.

The conflation of *u* and *v* is one of the main things you have to watch out for, when reading documents from that time, as in *haue* for *have*. The modern distinction between *i* and *j* had not been made either, so you find such unusual-looking spellings as *Iunes for Junes*.

Even 150 years later, in the time of Dr Johnson, we find hundreds of differences in the way words were spelled compared with today. Words ending in *-c* were spelled with *-ck*, as in *musick* and *publick*; and we find in Johnson's dictionary (1755) such spellings as *raindeer*, *villany* and *summersault*. Most nouns were given a capital letter, not just names of people and places. Here are the first two lines of Jonathan Swift's poem *Baucis and Philemon* (1706):

In antient Time, as Story tells
The Saints would often leave their Cells ...

The fashion to capitalize died out in print during the 18th century, but you will still find domestic letters peppered with capitals a century later.

Always expect to encounter some idiosyncratic uses of punctuation in any document over a century old. This is an 18th century example: *The answer to the question, is to be found in his writing.* We no longer put a comma between the subject and the verb in a sentence, even if we would insert a pause in speech.

Also notable are differences in vocabulary. Thousands of words have gone out of use, as in these from Johnson's dictionary: *merrythought* (= 'wishbone'), *fopdoodle* (= 'fool'), *nappiness* (= 'having a nap').

The letters of our grandparents and great-grandparents often contain puzzling expressions. Here are some you might find in the first decade of the 1900s: *deevy* (= 'delightful'), *hair-tidy* (= 'receptacle for hair combings'), *pip-pip* (= 'goodbye').

Grammar has changed too. If you read letters from the 1800s, you'll find yourself reading sentences like these. They are all perfectly understandable, but they sound quaintly archaic:

> *Father said we might keep the basket.*
> *That was where boats were used to be found.*
> *I have it not by me.*
> *Mayn't I go with you?*
> *It was quite too adorable.*

They are the kind of thing we might come across in a novel by Jane Austen.

Pronunciation has changed. The voices of the late 19th century sound very much like those of today – we have phonograph recordings from that time – except that some words are pronounced differently. They didn't say <u>bal</u>cony, in those days, but bal<u>cony</u> – 'bal-<u>coh</u>-nee'. A word like *lord* would have sounded more like 'lard', and *daughter* like 'darter'.

One of the most interesting experiments of the 2000s was the productions of two of Shakespeare's plays at Shakespeare's Globe in London in 'original pronunciation' – the accents that would have been used around the year 1600. How do we know? The chief evidence lies in the rhymes, puns, spellings and descriptions from contemporaries. Often when we read or see a Shakespeare play we encounter a pair of lines that are supposed to rhyme – but they don't. Here's an example, from Puck in *A Midsummer Night's Dream* (3.2.118):

> Then will two at once woo one –
> That must needs be sport alone

Today, *one* and *alone* don't rhyme, and the lines jar. In Shakespeare's day they would have rhymed: *one* was pronounced as 'own'. You can hear examples of how the speech would have sounded at the website www.originalpronunciation.com

47 Has internet technology changed English?

> The popular view is that there have been many changes. The reality is the opposite.

Not in any major way. The English we see on the internet now is mostly the same as we saw before digital technology arrived. There have been a few thousand new words and expressions, of course, but they are a drop in the lexical ocean of English, which contains well over a million words (see **1**). I don't see anything happening to grammar online that isn't happening offline. The most noticeable developments have been in orthography, where we see new writing styles that are departures from Standard English, such as punctuation minimalism (with marks being omitted in informal contexts) and maximalism (with marks being used excessively). A message saying *That's great news* would in Standard English contain a capital letter, an apostrophe, and a final period. In an email or social forum we might see it with no capitalization and punctuation at all; or it might end with multiple exclamation marks!!!!!

The new technology does occasionally introduce usages that weren't there before – sometimes very unpredictably. The fact that we have instant messaging now, with applications like WhatsApp, presents a new dynamic among the people using it that has immediate linguistic consequences, such as sentences becoming shorter and a sentence sequence broken down into separate messages, often separated by interventions from the recipient. Period omission is routine, because its two main functions are no longer needed. It is visually obvious when a short statement has come to an end. And as most interactions are single sentences, its function as a sentence-separator is also redundant.

But if the stylistic norm is now *not* to use a period at the end of statements in messaging, this opens up the possibility that its presence means something special – and this is what has happened. Adding a period adds an emotional charge to the interaction. There is a semantic contrast between:

Kim's coming to the party tonight

which means simply that Kim is coming to the party, and:

Kim's coming to the party tonight.

which means something like 'oh dear', 'I wasn't expecting that', or some other serious implication. The period in English (and I suppose in other languages) has never had that kind of emotive function before.

This isn't solely a young person's usage. Many older people now omit periods in instant messaging, and sense a difference when someone puts one in. In a small corpus of interactions I collected, I noticed that some of the writers would add a period when they were about to sign off (as in 'Talk again soon.' 'Have to go now.'). It seemed to show they had nothing more to say.

These are trends, not rules, but well worth exploring with learners. Indeed, to keep up to date, we have no alternative. The practices that young people are intuitively recognizing or evolving themselves are very different from the rules that older people know. So this is where it's very important to gather as much data as we can to tap into current intuitions about what's going on.

For instance, there was a study done a little while ago on the use of ellipsis dots (...) in messaging. For me, these dots simply mean that something has been left out or left unfinished. So if I send a message to you saying, 'How's it going ...?' I'm just being informal. But a youngster receiving this message would often read in a different implication: 'What is it about me that he has in mind?', perhaps, or 'Am I in some sort of trouble?' The dots imply a serious intent behind the question. I have no personal intuition about this. I can get a sense of this kind of change only by talking to young people. And I am always prepared to be surprised.

Will text messaging harm my learners' English?

The short answer is no. My answer explains why.

Texting had a bad press. People thought that the written language seen on mobile phone screens was new and alien. It was labelled 'textese', 'slanguage', a 'digital virus', and described as 'foreign' and 'outlandish'. Young people were said to fill their messages with newfangled abbreviations that they had invented to prevent adults from understanding what they were saying. They left letters out of words, showing that they didn't know how to spell. They were putting the abbreviations into their essays and exam scripts. In short, the texting generation was marking the beginning of an unprecedented decline in the English language.

All these popular beliefs were wrong. It was never used just by the young: the vast majority of texts circulating in cyberspace were among adults, and especially by and to institutions such as the stock-market and colleges. When linguists began to compile corpora of texts for analysis, it emerged that only a tiny number used a distinctive orthography. The abbreviations weren't totally new. Young people didn't use them in essays or exams. And when psychologists began to look into text messaging they showed that texting helped rather than hindered literacy.

In any collection of texts, it was the combination of standard and nonstandard features which was the most striking characteristic – and with good reason. Although many texters liked to be different, and enjoyed breaking linguistic rules, they also knew they needed to be understood. What was the point in sending a message to someone if it broke so many rules that it ceased to be intelligible? There was always an unconscious pressure to use the standard orthography.

The research studies made it perfectly clear that the early media hysteria about the novelty (and thus the dangers) of text messaging was misplaced. In one American study, less than 20 percent of the texts showed abbreviated forms of any kind. In my own collection, the figure was about 10 percent. And few of the abbreviations were novel. Forms such as *C* ('see'), *U* ('you') and *2* ('to') were popular in the 19th century. The use of initial letters for whole words (*n* 'no', *cmb* 'call me back') is even earlier: *IOU*, for example, is known from 1618. And forms with letters omitted, such as *msg* ('message'), weren't new either. Eric Partridge published a *Dictionary of Abbreviations* in 1942 which contained dozens of examples, such as *agn* 'again' and *gd* 'good'.

Texters did use deviant spellings – but they knew they were deviant. They wouldn't have been able to use mobile phone technology at all if they hadn't been taught to read and write, which means they all had a grounding in the Standard English writing system. But they were by no means the first to use such nonstandard forms as *cos* 'because' or *wot* 'what'. Several are so much part of English literary tradition that they've been given entries in the *Oxford English Dictionary*. *Cos* is there from 1828 and *wot* from 1829. Many can be found in literary dialect representations, such as by Charles Dickens and Mark Twain.

You'll notice I've been using the past tense in this piece. The novelty of those abbreviations has worn off. A little while ago, I visited a school where the learners had collected some of their text messages for analysis. There wasn't a single abbreviation to be seen. I asked them where they had gone, and they looked at me oddly. 'They aren't cool any more,' was the reply. There are several reasons. Predictive text makes it much easier not to abbreviate. And one lad said to me, 'I stopped abbreviating when my dad started'! When older people adopt young people's slang, it definitely is no longer cool!

Texting has certainly added a new dimension to language use, but its long-term impact on already existing varieties of language was negligible. It was never going to harm anyone.

49 Why are transcripts of spoken language so difficult to read?

> The differences between speech and writing are considerable, and often underestimated. This becomes clear when we try to write speech down.

'Spoken language' here has to mean spontaneous speech, especially of an informal kind, as in everyday conversation. Scripted speech, such as a news broadcast, doesn't usually present a problem, for the transcription is already there in the text being read. But writing down what happens in a real conversation is a very different matter. I stress *real*, not the simplified and carefully structured dialogues typical of coursebooks. Most of our linguistic lives are taken up with conversation, so it's important for learners to be given realistic accounts of what takes place, if they are to participate with good listening comprehension and make their own contributions in a stylistically appropriate way. That is where a transcription comes in.

Why is there a difficulty? The aim of a transcription is to replicate what's been said, so that, if someone were to read it aloud, the result would sound the same as the original – of course allowing for differences in voice quality and accent – and convey the same meaning. For that to happen, all the 'prosodic' features – intonation, loudness (including stress), rhythm, tempo and pause – have to be noted, as well as any 'tones of voice' (a conspiratorial whisper, for instance). The transcription becomes visually complex, as a result, and it takes training to become adept at reading it.

Anyone who's grappled with the intonation transcriptions in EFL books like O'Connor and Arnold's *Intonation of Colloquial English* will remember the problem – and those texts were very simplified. More complex, but still simplified, were the transcriptions that Derek Davy and I made for *Advanced Conversational English*. We used notes to tell readers about the features we omitted from the transcription. (The original book is long out of print, but an online version is now freely available from my website, along with the audio files.)

The alternative is to show no prosodic features at all, and to write down the words using conventional punctuation, but that produces a different kind of difficulty. The result is easier to read, but the dynamic of speech is missing. Punctuation is a poor guide to prosody. And many utterances become challenging to interpret, such as *so I was like ready for whatever you know I think they were going to ask me*. We can put in commas or dashes to show the structure (*so, I was, like, ready for whatever, you know, I think they were going to ask me*), but that makes the utterance look totally non-fluent, whereas in reality it sounded smooth and natural.

As this example illustrates, spontaneous speech isn't like writing. It contains long, loosely constructed sentences, often with many clauses linked by *and*. Speakers have sudden changes of thought, leaving one sentence unfinished and starting a new one. They use expressions such as *you know* and *you see* (what are often called *comment clauses*) to keep their speech flowing. They blend constructions which would be corrected in writing, and which would be called 'wrong' in teaching (such as *Yes, I've seen her three weeks ago*). The vocabulary may be vague, even to the point of using 'nonsense words' such as *thingummy*, when the speaker can't bring a word to mind. And on top of all that, there are the interruptions and overlapping speech by the participants.

None of this would be noticed in the normal give-and-take of everyday speech, but when it's written down in a transcript, the contrast with conventional written language can be dramatic. All the written language you've ever read – in books, magazines, newspapers – has been edited, with copy-editors and proofreaders eliminating infelicities. There's just one exception: online. When people write a blog or a tweet, or contribute to a social media forum, there's no copy-editor watching over them. They tend to write as they speak. It's the closest you can get to seeing spoken language in printed form.

How can English usage protect you from being robbed online? Read this, and stay safe.

Phishing was coined as a clever play on words. It's the fraudulent attempt to obtain sensitive information from you about your online passwords, credit card numbers, bank account details, and so on, chiefly by impersonating a genuine company. It derives from *fishing* – literally, the art and practice of catching fish, but used figuratively since the 16th century for any artifice that gets information from someone, as in *He was fishing around for news of the election*. We receive a message whose graphic design replicates the house style of a company and therefore looks totally plausible.

Is it possible to identify a fraudulent message from the language it uses? This is the kind of enquiry that is carried out routinely in forensic linguistics. As with any genre recognized by its distinctive language, a stylistic analysis would be able to identify the salient features – as has often taken place in relation to science, law, religion and other special domains, as well as many literary styles. In the case of phishing, the task is complicated by the fact that the messages come from people with very different backgrounds and countries, with a varying command of the language in which they phish. But that in itself can provide a clue.

A genuine organization will have people whose job it is to ensure that the language it uses in official communications, online or offline, is in Standard English. Phishing messages typically don't take such care, so the presence of nonstandard English is an immediate clue to the dubious origins of a message. There will be pointers of nonstandard spelling, punctuation and grammar, as well as awkwardness of style and inconsistency (such as in the use of capital letters). Here are two examples, with the nonstandard, awkward and inconsistent features underlined:

> We have received several <u>complaint</u> from users unable to gain access to their email account<u>,</u> as a result of <u>that</u>, we are upgrading our

security systems and making sure each user <u>a</u>ccount is not <u>accessed</u> <u>unauthorised.</u> We do not want you to <u>loose</u> access to your <u>A</u>ccount since your login <u>information are</u> no longer valid on our database system.

This is <u>an important information</u> regarding your Google account. We have just realized that your account <u>i</u>nformation on our database system is out of date, <u>as a result of that</u> we request <u>that you to</u> <u>verifyy</u> our <u>I</u>nformation by <u>filling your account information</u> below.

What we are seeing in these examples is the emerging role of nonstandard English as an index of internet illegitimacy.

There is an interesting implication here for ELT. Normally, nonstandard English is mentioned as something to be avoided at all costs, unless well-justified, such as when we encounter characters in a play or novel who speak in that way. But here we see a reason for taking a serious interest in nonstandard language. Of course, to recognize the relevant features presupposes that the learner has reached a sufficient level in Standard English to be able to see the differences. But it isn't necessary to detect all the errors, nor to introduce them all at once.

For instance, when teaching the difference between countable and uncountable nouns (see **15**), typical errors (such as *an information*) are bound to be mentioned. That would be an opportune moment to mention the way these forms turn up in phishing. Similarly, we might point out examples of wrong noun number (*complaint*), concord (*information are*), or verb confusion (*loose/lose*) at the appropriate points in the syllabus. This would help sharpen the distinction between standard and nonstandard in the learners' minds, as well as increase their awareness and understanding of the dangers they can encounter online.

Studying English usage isn't just interesting and pedagogically useful, it seems. One day it might actually save you from being robbed!

Index

Entries in *italics* refer to information about usage of that word in English, for example, '*dialect*' (the word) as well as 'dialects' (as subject).